PR   Wade, Bryan, 1950-
9199.3
.W314 Blitzkrieg, and
B54   other plays

BLITZKRIEG

and other plays

bryan Wade

alias
lifeguard
underground
electric gunfighters

PLAYWRIGHTS PRESS

CAUTION: These plays are fully protected under the copyright laws of Canada, and all other countries of the Copyright Union, and are subject to royalty. Changes to any script are expressly forbidden without written consent of the author. Rights to produce, film or record in whole or in part in any medium or in any language, by any group, AMATEUR or PROFESSIONAL, are retained by the author. Interested persons are requested to apply for permission and terms to:

> Great North Agency
> Suite 500
> 345 Adelaide Street West
> Toronto Canada M5V 1R5
> 416-363-9901

Published with the generous assistance of the Canada Council, the Ontario Arts Council, the Ontario Ministry of Culture and Recreation, Alberta Culture, Metropolitan Toronto and the City of Toronto.

Playwrights Press (a division of Playwrights Canada)
8 York Street
Toronto, Canada
M5J 1R2
416-363-1581

Cover design by Peggy Livingston
Cover photograph of Bryan Wade by Don MacLean

Typeset by Betterback Ltd., Toronto
Printed in Canada by Johanns Graphics, Waterloo

ISBN 0-88754-122-4
First Edition: August 1979

This one is for Donna

CONTENTS

INTRODUCTION

Northrop Frye has suggested that the Canadian sensibility is shaped not so much by a quest for identity, but by an attempt to locate the environment: "Where is here?" The documentary tradition — as evidenced in such manifestations as the work of the National Film Board and even Pierre Berton's pop histories — appears as one of the mainstream approaches to answering that question. It comes as no surprise, then, to find that much of our contemporary theatre is preoccupied with documentary form. The success of *The Farm Show, Ten Lost Years* and *Paper Wheat,* among many others, testifies to our fascination with seeing "real people in real situations". No doubt viewing the manners and morals of Newfoundland seal hunters, Depression housewives and hockey players does help to define just where "here" is, but the popularity of the form suggests a disquieting corollary: that the Canadian sensibility distrusts the imagination. The artist who chooses to present a personal vision and create structures that originate with an intuited sense of life generally finds a hostile reception.

Even outside the documentary genre, the most widely produced playwrights seem to be those whose vision is bound by traditional dramaturgy and/or naturalistic premises. Thus, the playwright who truly makes things up, who creates characters and situations far removed from the recognizable world of, say, prairie mental asylums, is in for tough sledding around the old beaver lodge.

Bryan Wade makes things up, and this collection of some of his early work suggests why he should be considered one of our major theatrical voices. The people in these plays have no counterparts in the work of other contemporary playwrights: Adolf Hitler marshalling rats into his service, the Lone Ranger riding a penis. They are original images, and coupled with dramatic structures that tend to minimize narrative, they create a world that reflects a strong and unique talent. There is probably little chance that plays of such an idiosyncratic temperament will garner wide popular appeal. *Blitzkrieg,* for example, would not do big box office in Winnipeg's North End for the Manitoba Theatre Centre. Nonetheless, those willing to let Wade take them where his mind does wander are in for true theatrical experiences.

II

The three short plays collected here, *Electric Gunfighters, Lifeguard* and *Alias,* are early works and appear somewhat derivative in style. However, all three possess a sharp theatrical sense and establish some of the concerns that are to engage Wade in his later work.

Lifeguard is the kind of surreal allegory most young playwrights feel compelled to write in an attempt to explain The Nature of Existence. In this one, a lifeguard tries to protect a couple caught up in the dynamics of their relationship from no less a fate than Death itself, here construed as two swimmers lurking offshore. Although the piece seems loaded down by Significant Ideas, *Lifeguard* possesses a particularly vibrant set of images. The dirty beach with its extraordinary bugs, and Ernie's stories about the dead dog and the child defecating, create a specific and resonant atmosphere. The relationship between Ernie and Lorraine is built on tension that has the struggle for sexual power at its root, and although the situation is barely explored here, it presents a preliminary sketch for a number of couples we are to find in the sexual war zone in later plays.

Electric Gunfighters has two young men playing out routines cribbed from every horse opera to hit the screen. Bob and Pete are wired to the images of Western movies and engage in shoot-out after shoot-out in what first appears as jovial play-acting. It becomes apparent, though, that the boys have been virtually "sucked in there by a huge vacuum cleaner" and their synapses have been fried by too much TV. The point is obvious, of course, and this obsession with media and technology is to become more and more a central concern of Wade's. The play is also notable for its witty appropriation of the Western vernacular; it keeps the play clipping along in a whimsical tone that sets up the final revelation with a nice ironic touch.

Alias, which appears here in a recently revised version, is the most accomplished of these one-acts. It is also cast within a media image of the Wild West, but whereas *Electric Gunfighters* focused on the way we respond to the idealizations of behaviour offered by the cowboy melodrama, *Alias* takes an imaginative leap into the consciousness of the mythic hero. Wade cops the figures of the Lone Ranger and Tonto, sets them in new characterizations and creates a situation designed to send up the myth and articulate some neat observations about the nature of heroism. The original Lone Ranger narrative — with its images of the individualistic white vigilante defending Virtue, Justice and the Republic, aided by the loyal and "trustworthy" (read subjugated) red man — is surely one of the most transparent metaphors for the American experience. In *Alias,* Wade turns the images inside out. The Lone Ranger becomes a bumbling adolescent, so caught up in playing Sir Galahad that he is totally distanced from himself. Tonto, no longer the laconic cigar store Indian popularized by Jay Silverheels, emerges as a self-aware, prairie-wise champion of the truly noble. Wade has comically debunked the Lone Ranger myth by simply reversing the roles and making Tonto the character with the real strength.

In the midst of this identity crisis, Wade introduces another archetypal figure — the "femme fatale". Rebecca appears virtually as a projection of the Ranger's inadequacies, and her attempts to seduce (i.e. control) both the Lone Ranger and Tonto outline the other major theme of the piece: the acceptance of sexuality. While saving Rebecca, i.e. "playing" the Lone Ranger, our hero is totally unreceptive to Rebecca's come-on. He is blithely ignorant of any sexual role, as if the Lone Ranger persona and its heroic straightjacket precludes any normal human response. In effect, Wade seems to be saying that this idealization of masculine behaviour, despite all its rootin'-tootin' bravado, isn't really a man at all, but indeed just a mask. Wade brilliantly underscores this idea with the appearance of a penis that wanders into the action. The ambulatory organ turns out to be Amy, a saloon gal trapped in a gimmicky costume by Rebecca, but the image plays as the Ranger's sublimated sexual/human self. And it's not until the sleep-walking scene, where the Ranger rides the penis and reveals his Lady of the Lake-like dream, that our hero shows any sign of resolving his problems.

Tonto, of course, is able to resist Rebecca's various charms because he knows who he is, what his feelings are, and possesses an instinctive sense of the way things should be. He's a perfect noble savage, and though Wade takes delight in parodying the archetype, the character is more than just a cartoon caricature. Here Tonto acts not just because his role is to help the Ranger, but because his sense of justice and friendship, established by Wade as bonafide, demands that he act in an honest, human way.

Implicit in the play is the fact that the Ranger's crisis is our fault — we who would invest a cowboy with a black mask and mythic stature. *Alias* is as much about the demands we make on our heroes as with delineating the identity theme. Here Rebecca also functions as an exploiter, desirous of using the Lone Ranger, Tonto and Amy for her own ends. And it is only Tonto's virtue and savvy that manage to repulse her threat and save the day for all concerned. In the end, the Ranger seems to be on the way to some kind of self-actualization. But he's still in limbo — no longer the Lone Ranger, he's in transition, just "Alias" — and we are left to speculate as to whether or not he will eventually succeed in finding himself.

Alias works because Wade audaciously takes on the whole Freudian analysis of behaviour, sets it up as comedy, and lets us laugh our way through the Lone Ranger's crisis. The play delights in blatantly establishing the characters as not only figures in a mythic landscape but also as types from the psychological interpretative system. The major points of the classic adolescent identity crisis model are laid bare in a witty, ironic reflection on heroes and myth-making. Wade is able to theatricalize all these elements in such a way that the piece holds together as a resonant fantasy. *Alias* is almost a perfect one-acter. It makes its point in concise characterizations, a direct action, and sure-fire theatrical images.

III

Blitzkrieg is Bryan Wade's first major play, and it marks the emergence of a truly personal style and a sophisticated technique that is found only in embryo in the one-acts. Here Wade's ability to formulate a dynamic interchange between character and image, in order to create a meaning-laden theatrical structure, becomes formidably apparent. In this reverie, which takes the shape of ''a play about Hitler and Eva'', the playwright discovers the power of the theatre to induce states of consciousness that radically affect an audience, and forces us to reformulate our conventional ways of interpreting reality.

The premise of *Blitzkrieg* is founded on a marvellous conceit. Wade appropriates the figures of Adolf Hitler and Eva Braun, not for the sake of biography, but in order to use our preconceptions about these people in a calculated attempt to build a new way of looking at romance and power. The appeal of real-life personages is obvious. We all want to know what Adolf Hitler is ''really like'', as the off-stage lives of the celebrated seem to be eternally fascinating. This is Wade's hook. He manipulates our curiosity about Hitler, and aptly casts us as voyeurs into the private life of the Fuhrer and his mistress. Implicit in the premise of *Blitzkrieg* is the knowledge that we are watching Adolf and Eva fucking on the ashes of six million Jews, and it is the sheer obscenity of this image that rivets us to the action of the play.

Given the power of the voyeur situation, Wade wastes little time in giving us what we've come for. The major scenes of the play are the two seductions — one initiated by Eva, the other by Adolf. Both are power plays, and the imagery is harsh, the behaviour cruel and manipulative: Hitler crawling on the floor; Eva grinding her heel into his back; Adolf pointing a gun into the groin of the spread-eagled Eva; talk of the world in holocaust; and the most hallucinatory image in all of these plays — Eva goose-stepping about the stage screaming ''Orgasm!'' Needless to say, all of this is extremely visceral, almost outrageous, and it appears as one of the most powerful statements on the relationship between sex and power to emerge in our theatre.

Even more potent, though, is the realization that this relationship is predicated on true affection. *Blitzkrieg* is a love story, the playing off of two romantic visions of the world against one another. For both Eva and Hitler are dreamers, and the sexual struggle at the core of the play has to do with each trying to coerce the other into the role demanded by their respective fantasies. Eva wants Hitler to be John Barrymore to her Greta Garbo. Hitler will have none of that: ''There's no place for their kind of love in the world''. On the other hand, Hitler wants Eva to totally submit her will to his — in the extreme case, to kill herself for him. And she's botched the job. This curious mixture of perverse sexual behaviour, and the almost naïve romantic fantasies it is based upon, gives the play its tension. And it is this tension, transferred to us as voyeurs, that constitutes the drama of *Blitzkrieg*.

Stylistically, the play is a significant development from the one-acts. Wade has always made us aware of his plays as theatre: characters tend to perform for one another (and us) and the playwright makes no attempt to disguise that fact in naturalistic form. In *Blitzkrieg,* as well as casting us as voyeurs, Wade surrounds us with imagery that reinforces the sense of theatre. The play is about fantasy, and *is* a fantasy. As Hitler says: ''You should remember that they're actors saying their lines. They're posing as people who don't really exist''. Just like Garbo and Barrymore in *Grand Hotel*, Eva's belief that she is an actress, or Hitler's ''perfect control'' in Eva's photographs, all is illusion. So too is Bryan Wade's Hitler and Eva. But the fact that they don't exist, doesn't make them any less *real*. Which would seem to be the point of *Blitzkrieg*. Power, sex, Hitler's rats, Eva's dream of Berghof: all are real, and their reality is only limited by the individual's ability to dream and to sustain the dream — to transform imagination into experience. If you are really good at it, you too can be Adolf Hitler.

IV

''You have to know how to control your breath when you're in the deep end'', says Gerry in *Underground*, and in this bleak and frightening foray into psychological warfare, Wade attempts breath control through a novel, non-dramatic form. Essentially a *Rashomon*-like situation, Wade presents an identical encounter three times. The characters change, but the elements of the action are the same: interrogation, denial, retreat, sexual encounter, violence and defeat. Because the script seems to dangle clues such as: ''what it's all about'', it's tempting to see the play as a puzzle: the successful putting-together of the pieces resulting in the meaning. However, *Underground* has no real narrative. Al, Gerry and Claire certainly operate as characters — they are people who are involved with each other — but it is important to see their encounters as self-contained. The play is a series of moments between two people, with occasional references to the third, and it is in the nature of the individual moments that the play is centred.

Thematically, *Underground* paints a despairing vision of our inability to find constancy in relationships. As Al says, ''I don't believe in anything any more. I expect everything to be false''. The characters are isolated in their personal obsessions: Al with the subway and life underground, Claire with her walks and life on the surface, Gerry with time, his tape recorder and flying — life above ground. What we are witnessing is the intransigence of these people in their positions and the attempt of each to press his version of reality on the other. It's a stalemate in all three scenes, and it is only the force of a stronger personality that provokes movement. Meanwhile, they put each other through vicious sadomasochistic routines that for force of cruelty are among Wade's most intense scenes.

Seeing this play is exhausting for an audience. *Underground* cuts deep because it focuses attention on detail — the inflection of a voice, a slip of the tongue, the thing not said — in short, the stuff that makes and breaks relationships. *Underground* leaves you numb, suspicious and lost: ''You have to protect yourself these days. I don't believe in my past . . . I don't know if it really happened or if I just thought it did. I can't trust my imagination any more''.

Wade's attempt at setting all of this in an objective, non-linear form is his most radical essay in theatrical form to date. By denying us the security of conventional dramatic form, Wade places us in a situation not dissimilar from that of the characters: searching for a foot-hold. Everything can be false, not only people, but also photographs, tape recordings and clocks. In *Underground*, even the devices we use to objectify experience can mislead, and so we are caught in a world without referents, where, like Al, the only things we can really believe in are those we are experiencing at the moment they take place.

As is the case with most attempts at experimental form, however, the very novelty of the style calls attention to the structure. As a result, our attention to the details of the experience exposed in *Underground* is diverted by the devices set up to establish the parallel situations. For example, the photograph which has three different compositions tends to upstage the events that it commemorates. Although we accept the premise that it can be perceived in three different ways, we still want to know what the photograph really looks like. This hangover from our expectations of conventional dramatic structures tends to lessen the impact of the play. Wade wants us to see things in a new way, but like African natives seeing movies for the first time, we don't know the rules of the game. So for all the genuine power in the moment-to-moment movement of the play, *Underground* appears as less than the sum of its parts, mainly because we are unfamiliar with such a radical re-ordering of experience. Still, *Underground* is a major theatrical achievement, and a script that will reveal more and more in productions to come. The play attempts to redefine the dramatic vocabulary, and the extent to which it is able to render depth of feeling in a new way suggests the strength of Bryan Wade's talent.

V

These five plays offer a wealth of vibrant images and themes, moving all the way from the television-blitzed Bob and Pete of *Electric Gunfighters* to the experience-wracked Al, Gerry and Claire of *Underground*. In each case, Wade seizes upon a very particular vision of life, shapes it with carefully chosen characters and generally succeeds in making his point with humour, insight and compassion. In the plays that have appeared since *Underground*, be it the Twilight Zone mystery of *This Side of the Rockies*, the troubled domesticity of *Tanned* or the star-crossed romance of *Breakthrough*, Wade continues to stretch his talent and provide new images and challenges for our theatre and for the Canadian sensibility. In providing his answers to Frye's "Where is here?", Bryan Wade enriches our experience and charts an imaginative life that makes our theatre a better place.

Bob White
Factory Theatre Lab
Toronto, 1979

lifeguard

12

CHARACTERS

LIFEGUARD, mid-twenties

ERNIE, early forties

LORRAINE, Ernie's wife, early forties

SWIMMERS, a young man and young woman, whose bodies are
            completely white

A beach. The Lifeguard's chair is centred on the stage. An overturned
rowboat lies beside his chair.

LIFEGUARD was first produced by the New Play Centre at the
Vancouver Art Gallery in 1973.

LIFEGUARD

In the darkness you can hear rhythmic breathing. It is the Woman Swimmer giving artificial respiration to the Man Swimmer. Blue light comes on full, flooding the stage area. The Woman Swimmer keeps exhaling into his mouth, pausing to inhale more air.

The Lifeguard comes on, climbs up and sits in his chair. He wears a swim suit, a white sun helmet and a whistle hangs from his neck. He scans the audience with his binoculars. Then he puts the binoculars down and gives one long blast on the whistle.

LIFEGUARD: Let's go. Let's clear the beach.

The Swimmers look up at him, then the Woman Swimmer breathes into the Man Swimmer's mouth.

Come on. We don't have all day, you know.

The Swimmers stand, look at him.

Put your gear on and get off the beach. People will be here soon.

The Man Swimmer smiles, puts on his face mask and snorkel. The Lifeguard blows his whistle again.

I'll only say it once more. Come on, let's go. Let's clear the beach.

The Woman Swimmer smiles, puts on her face mask and snorkel.

The Swimmers go off.

ERNIE: *(off)* I don't know why we have to bring so much stuff.

LORRAINE: *(off)* Because we need it.

ERNIE: *(off)* The idea of a holiday is to relax.

Ernie comes on, carrying a lawnchair and a beach umbrella. Lorraine follows him, carrying a beach bag. Ernie wears a short-sleeved shirt and shorts.

LORRAINE: And that's what we're going to do.

ERNIE: Where do you want it?

LORRAINE: This place looks as good as any. *(she points)* Put it right there.

Ernie puts the umbrella down and folds out the lawnchair.

ERNIE: How's that?

LORRAINE: Pull it farther down.

Ernie pulls the lawnchair a couple of feet downstage.

LORRAINE: Perfect.

ERNIE: Where should I put the umbrella?

LORRAINE: Wherever you like.

> *Lorraine takes off her dress. She wears a one-piece bathing suit. Ernie opens the umbrella, plants it downstage right. Lorraine stretches out in the lawnchair.*

I'm going to get a good tan today.

ERNIE: It looks like it'll be nice.

LIFEGUARD: It sure does.

> *Ernie turns, looks up at the Lifeguard.*

ERNIE: I didn't notice you. I thought we'd be the first ones on the beach today.

LIFEGUARD: You have to get up early to beat us.

ERNIE: I guess so.

LORRAINE: Who are you talking to?

ERNIE: The Lifeguard.

> *Lorraine turns, waves at the Lifeguard.*

LORRAINE: Hello!

LIFEGUARD: Hello!

> *Lorraine lies back in her chair.*

ERNIE: I'm glad you're around in case there's any trouble.

LIFEGUARD: We try to do our best. But sometimes . . .

ERNIE: What?

LIFEGUARD: *(confidentially)* Mistakes happen. Last week a young couple drowned.

ERNIE: You don't say.

LIFEGUARD: They were swimming out by that patch of weeds. And the next time I looked, they were gone.

ERNIE: You never know when it can happen. They say your whole life passes before your eyes as you drown.

LIFEGUARD: Yeah. They do say that.

ERNIE: I wonder if it happened to them. If they saw everything over again.

> *Ernie goes to the beach bag and gets out a pair of binoculars. He scans the ocean.*

LORRAINE: I'm hot already.

ERNIE: Did you hear what happened? A young couple drowned last week. Boy, you sure wouldn't catch me way out there.

LORRAINE: I'm really hot. I think my legs are burning.

ERNIE: Then move into the shade.

LORRAINE: But I have to get my tan.

ERNIE: Then don't.

Pause. Ernie is still scanning.

LORRAINE: Ernie.

ERNIE: What?

LORRAINE: How would you like to give me a rubdown? You're so good at it.

ERNIE: I'm busy right now.

LORRAINE: Doing what?

ERNIE: I'm looking at the patch of weeds.

LORRAINE: They aren't there any more.

ERNIE: I know that.

LORRAINE: Too bad we weren't here last week. You could have watched them drag for the bodies.

ERNIE: *(lowering the binoculars)* You shouldn't talk like that.

LORRAINE: Maybe you could have saved the girl.

ERNIE: I doubt it.

LORRAINE: I can see it now. Her first cry for help, you dive into the water, swim furiously, grab her hand as she sinks for the last time. Then with your arm around her, you stroke powerfully with your legs —

ERNIE: Lorraine.

LORRAINE: — back to the shore. You carry her up the beach, lay her on the sand, give her mouth-to-mouth respiration. Her blue eyes open slowly . . .

ERNIE: That's his job.

LORRAINE: . . . she's trembling. You saved my life, she says.

ERNIE: The Lifeguard would have saved her if he could.

LORRAINE: I'm sure he would have. *(pause)* He's in such good shape.

ERNIE: That's how they all are.

LORRAINE: No one kicks sand in his face, eh Ernie?

ERNIE: He can hear what you're saying.

LORRAINE: I don't care. It's so nice just to look at him. Every time he moves he gives me goose-bumps.

She walks to the Lifeguard's chair.

I bet all the girls tell you how good-looking you are.

LIFEGUARD: A few, ma'am.

LORRAINE: How do you do it?

LIFEGUARD: Do what, ma'am?

LORRAINE: Stay so nice.

LIFEGUARD: We keep in training all the time, ma'am.

LORRAINE: Call me Lorraine. You know. You remind me of those Greek gods. The bronze ones. Remember all those statues we saw in the museum in Greece, Ernie?

ERNIE: All I remember is the heartburn I got from that shiskastick.

LORRAINE: Shishkabob, you mean. *(to Lifeguard)* I bet no one has said that about you.

LIFEGUARD: No, Lorraine.

LORRAINE: Would you mind moving for me?

LIFEGUARD: Moving what?

LORRAINE: Anything at all. Your biceps. Your head. Your big toe. Anything will do. Think of it as a favour for me.

> *After a moment the Lifeguard crosses his legs.*

LIFEGUARD: How's that?

LORRAINE: Fantastic. It really was.

ERNIE: I'll rub you down, Lorraine.

LORRAINE: *(to Lifeguard)* Thank you very much.

LIFEGUARD: You're welcome.

ERNIE: You'll burn if you don't get some oil.

LORRAINE: *(to Lifeguard)* I bet you'd like to hear about my dog.

ERNIE: He doesn't want to hear about that!

LORRAINE: How do you know?

ERNIE: Cause I do! Now come on. I'll rub you down.

LIFEGUARD: What about your dog?

LORRAINE: You see. I knew he wanted to hear about it.

ERNIE: He's only being polite!

LIFEGUARD: Oñ the contrary, I'm always interested in what people have to say.

> *Ernie, angry, sits in the lawnchair.*

LORRAINE: You'd be walking down the street or in a department store and people would stop and tell you how beautiful he was. He was well trained too. None of this doing what he felt like doing. Animals want discipline, so they can get your love. Our dog could do anything. He'd heel without you saying a word. He'd sit, shake a paw and fetch. He loved swimming out after a stick. It didn't matter how far you threw it cause he'd get it. And you should have seen him play dead. He'd do it for hours and not move a muscle. Not until you said the word.

> *Ernie takes a bottle of suntan lotion out of the beach bag and goes to Lorraine.*

He would talk to me. He'd bark and howl when he wanted to tell me something. And some people call them stupid.

Ernie puts suntan lotion on her shoulders.

I always understood what he said. He had different barks for when he was hungry, when he wanted to go outside for a run.

ERNIE: Let me give you a rubdown.

LORRAINE: All right. We had such a nice dog, didn't we?

ERNIE: The best in the world.

Ernie guides her back to the lawnchair.

She sits in it.

LORRAINE: And he was beautiful, wasn't he?

ERNIE: Very beautiful. Very smart.

She lies back in the chair. Ernie puts oil on her legs.

ERNIE: Now we'll put some oil on your legs.

LORRAINE: Okay.

ERNIE: Cause we want to get a tan.

LORRAINE: That's what we want.

ERNIE: Cause we're here to have a good time.

LORRAINE: We're on our holidays.

ERNIE: Now a little dab on your nose.

LORRAINE: That tickles.

ERNIE: There. You won't burn in a thousand years.

LORRAINE: I'm awful tired, Ernie.

ERNIE: Maybe you should have a nap.

LORRAINE: Yes.

ERNIE: Close your eyes and then you'll feel a lot better.

Lorraine closes her eyes.

LORRAINE: Feel a lot better.

ERNIE: It's the best thing for you.

LORRAINE: Best thing.

Ernie watches her for a moment.

LIFEGUARD: *(quietly)* She going to sleep?

Ernie nods his head. He walks up to the Lifeguard.

ERNIE: We went farther down the beach yesterday. Where there usually aren't too many people. Maybe I had drifted off to sleep for an hour. I heard a woman say, you'll be a good boy, won't you? Twenty feet from us there was a woman and her kid. He had his pants down and was squatting in the sand

and she had hold of his dink and was shaking it. Christ, the kid was trying like crazy to do something. This went on for about five minutes, her baby talking to him, the kid straining and grunting and trying as hard as he could until finally he dropped two small turds on the sand. But she wasn't satisfied with that. Don't you have to do a number one? Shake, shake. You can do better than that. Shake, shake. You sure that's all you have to do? But the kid was finished and he ran to the ocean with his pants around his knees. She caught him before he got to the water, pulled up his pants and walked away, dragging the kid behind her. She should have been arrested for that.

LIFEGUARD: She wouldn't have done it on my beach.

ERNIE: Course not. Sure, we all like taking a leak in the ocean when you go for a swim.

LIFEGUARD: You don't.

ERNIE: I don't do it that often. But not the beach. No wonder every grain of sand stinks here. And the bugs drive you crazy. There's millions of them.

LIFEGUARD: You mean fleas?

ERNIE: No, bugs.

LIFEGUARD: Cause every beach has sand fleas. Even this one.

ERNIE: I'm talking about bugs. Yesterday I passed a dog on the beach and bugs were crawling all over him. I pushed him over with a stick and there was a gaping hole in his side. They must have gone down through his mouth and eaten their way through from the inside. I hit him with my stick and you should have seen them jump. I hit him again and again. *(Ernie slaps himself)* Gotcha! *(he tries to pick the bug off his arm)* Jump off me, will you?

> *He bends down and picks up the bug between his fingers.*

You sure won't get me now.

> *Ernie dunks the bug in the ocean.*

How did you like that? Let's go in again. Had enough now? Say, there's a crab. I bet he'd like you. Sure he would. Come on, crab. Come and get it. A little closer. *(he gives the bug to the crab)* Chew him up. Good, eh? You bet he's good. And there's more where he came from. There's millions of them.

> *Ernie crawls around on the sand, looking for bugs. The Life-guard scans the ocean with his binoculars.*

You wait there. I'll have one for you in no time at all. Here's a nice big juicy one for you.

> *Ernie sees the Lifeguard is looking at something. He sits back on his heels and shades his eyes as he looks out at the ocean.*

Isn't there something moving out there?

LIFEGUARD: Yeah.

> *Ernie stands, walks to the edge of the shore, still looking.*

ERNIE: What is it?

LIFEGUARD: A log.

ERNIE: Seems to be moving too fast for that. *(pause)* It looks like someone swimming.

> *Ernie gets his binoculars from under the umbrella, scans the ocean with them.*

LIFEGUARD: Couldn't be. Current's too strong. They wouldn't last a minute.

ERNIE: He's gone!

LIFEGUARD: You mean it sank.

ERNIE: He was swimming!

LIFEGUARD: It happens all the time. Logs drift around, then all of a sudden they sink.

ERNIE: He must be drowning!

LIFEGUARD: Logs don't drown.

ERNIE: I saw him with my eyes!

LIFEGUARD: Are you sure?

ERNIE: Sure I am!

LIFEGUARD: Maybe you need your eyes checked.

ERNIE: Maybe we need a new Lifeguard!

LIFEGUARD: So now you can do my job, eh?

ERNIE: I didn't say that —

LORRAINE: *(waking up)* What's all this yelling?

ERNIE: I saw a man swimming and then he drowned and the Lifeguard says he wasn't there and —

LORRAINE: Slow down, Ernie.

LIFEGUARD: There was a log and it sank. Long distances can play tricks on you.

ERNIE: It's not true, Lorraine!

LORRAINE: Why should he lie?

ERNIE: I don't know. All I know is what I saw.

LORRAINE: You've been out in the sun too long.

LIFEGUARD: Don't you think I'd swim out there if it was someone?

ERNIE: Yeah. I guess so.

LIFEGUARD: We're trained to always be on the alert. Every minute we're on duty, we're ready to go into action.

ERNIE: I know that. But . . .

LIFEGUARD: I'm here to warn people and keep them safe. I wouldn't be doing my job if I let them get out in deep water. It's a long way back to shore. What if they have too much beer at lunch and get a cramp? What if they panic? If you're too far out, no one can save you. Not even the best Lifeguard in the world.

LORRAINE: He's right, Ernie.

ERNIE: I guess I made a mistake. It sure looked like someone though.

Ernie sits under the beach umbrella.

LIFEGUARD: Take the couple that drowned last week. I told them to come back but they wouldn't listen. By the time I got out there, they'd gone under. I swam down, looked in the weeds, then I had to go up for air. I did it five times.

Lorraine stands in front of his chair.

LORRAINE: You must be brave.

LIFEGUARD: Not really. You've been listening to me?

LORRAINE: Every word.

LIFEGUARD: You know what I'm getting at?

LORRAINE: I know you're in good shape.

LIFEGUARD: This is important.

LORRAINE: I'll say it is.

LIFEGUARD: So you'd do what I told you?

LORRAINE: I'd do anything for you.

LIFEGUARD: If I had to warn you.

LORRAINE: Warn me? Against what?

LIFEGUARD: I don't know. Something could come up.

LORRAINE: There's nothing to worry about on the beach.

LIFEGUARD: You haven't been listening!

LORRAINE: Sure I have.

LIFEGUARD: You don't understand! What's the use talking to you! You're like a stone wall! I won't bother any more if this is all the thanks I get!

The Lifeguard turns in his chair and looks down the beach away from them.

Lorraine and Ernie look at each other, then at the Lifeguard.

LORRAINE: *(to Lifeguard)* I'm sorry.

Pause. Ernie crosses to her.

I'll do what you say.

Pause. Ernie whispers in her ear.

You think so?

Ernie nods his head, then whispers in her ear.

ERNIE: It might do the trick for him.

Ernie gets on his hands and knees.

Lorraine stands beside him.

LORRAINE: You ready now?

Ernie nods his head.

Okay. Sit!

Ernie sits back on his heels.

Now I want you to beg. I want you to show the Lifeguard how nice you can be.

Ernie sits up, like a dog begging. The Lifeguard sneaks a look at them, then looks down the beach.

Now give us a big bark.

Ernie barks.

And so loud. Now I want you to shake a paw. Come on.

He lifts up his right hand and Lorraine shakes it.

That's the way to shake it.

Ernie barks again.

(to the Lifeguard) Isn't he good? Have you ever seen anyone as good as him?

The Lifeguard pretends he is looking down the beach.

Lay down like you're supposed to.

Ernie lies down on his stomach.

Good. No one's as good as you are. No one in the whole world. Now let's show him what we can do. Roll over.

Ernie rolls over.

And again. Roll back this way.

Ernie rolls back to her.

That's it!

Lorraine hugs him.

Come on, give us a kiss. A nice big kiss!

Ernie licks her face. The Lifeguard watches them. He laughs to himself.

Give Lorraine another one.

Ernie keeps licking her face and he runs his hands along her legs.

Stop it! You're getting me all wet! I know you love me. I love you too! Yes, I do!

Ernie rolls onto his back with his legs and arms up in the air. Lorraine leans over, licks his face.

You like that? You want another one?

She licks his face again, rubs his belly.

I bet that feels good.

> *Ernie barks. The Lifeguard laughs out loud.*

LIFEGUARD: You're great!

LORRAINE: Lorraine doesn't forget when you've been good. I bet you want a lay down. Don't you?

> *Ernie barks.*

LIFEGUARD: You're as funny as hell!

> *Lorraine lies on top of Ernie.*

LORRAINE: We haven't had a lay down for a long time, have we?

> *Ernie puts his arms around her.*

ERNIE: No.

LIFEGUARD: Just hold on a minute.

> *Lorraine licks Ernie's face slowly, sensually.*

You'll have to stop that. It's against the rules.

ERNIE: We can't stop.

LORRAINE: Because we're having a lay down.

ERNIE: And we haven't had one for a long time.

LIFEGUARD: This is a public beach.

> *The Lifeguard blows his whistle.*

> *They're kissing, licking each other's faces.*

LORRAINE: Feels good.

ERNIE: Feels so good.

LIFEGUARD: You'll have to get up.

> *The Lifeguard blows his whistle as he stands in his chair.*

LORRAINE: Delicious.

ERNIE: Tasty too.

> *They kiss again. Ernie hooks his legs over Lorraine's thighs. They begin to rock back and forth. The Lifeguard climbs down from his chair.*

LIFEGUARD: You can't do things like that in broad daylight. If you get up now, we'll forget it happened. All right?

> *Ernie and Lorraine are rocking faster now.*

> *The Lifeguard blows his whistle loudly.*

Now break it up!

> *The Lifeguard takes hold of Lorraine by the shoulders.*

LIFEGUARD: Up you get!

LORRAINE: What are you doing?

The Lifeguard pulls her up off Ernie.

ERNIE: Hey!

LIFEGUARD: I warned you! I told you to stop.

LORRAINE: We were just getting started.

ERNIE: *(sitting up)* You can't stop us!

LIFEGUARD: No one can do everything they want all the time.

LORRAINE: Who gave you the right to tell us what to do?

> *Ernie stands, walks to the Lifeguard and pushes him in the chest.*

LIFEGUARD: I think you better sit down.

ERNIE: Don't want to fight me, eh?

> *Ernie pushes the Lifeguard in the chest again.*

LIFEGUARD: I won't ask you again.

LORRAINE: I think you better do what he says, Ernie.

ERNIE: This is one time I won't back down.

> *Ernie pushes him in the chest again.*
>
> *The Lifeguard takes hold of Ernie's hand and twists his arm behind his back.*

LIFEGUARD: I don't want to have to break it.

ERNIE: Let go of me!

> *The Lifeguard forces Ernie's arm higher up his back. Ernie cries out in pain.*

LORRAINE: Don't hurt him.

> *The Lifeguard marches Ernie to the umbrella, sits him down, lets go of his arm.*

ERNIE: I won't forget this, you know.

> *Lorraine comforts him.*

LORRAINE: You're a bully!

LIFEGUARD: Why don't we forget this happened and go back to what we were doing? This is your holiday. You're here to relax.

ERNIE: I'm going to report you!

> *Lorraine sits beside Ernie. The Lifeguard climbs into his chair. He picks up the binoculars and scans the ocean.*

LORRAINE: Did he hurt you a lot?

ERNIE: Hardly at all.

LIFEGUARD: Jesus!

LORRAINE: Were you afraid?

ERNIE: No. Well . . . maybe a little. But, Lorraine, I didn't care.

LIFEGUARD: They'll be coming in soon!

LORRAINE: I was proud of you.

LIFEGUARD: Leave while you still have the chance!

ERNIE: It was nice to have you close again.

LORRAINE: It was beautiful.

LIFEGUARD: Please, get out of here!

ERNIE: Do you hear someone?

LORRAINE: No.

> *The yellow light fades out as blue light fades in.*

LIFEGUARD: Ernie! Lorraine! They're coming in now!

ERNIE: Sounds like a carburetor to me.

LORRAINE: No, it sounds more like the garburetor is spitting out what it's chewed up.

LIFEGUARD: Look, I'm sorry about what I said.

LORRAINE: Do you want to play dead?

ERNIE: Not right now.

LIFEGUARD: Please, leave, while you still have the chance.

> *The blue light is up full now.*

LORRAINE: Come on. Do it for me.

ERNIE: Let's both play dead.

LORRAINE: I don't feel like it.

ERNIE: Then I won't either.

LIFEGUARD: *(imploring)* You said you'd listen. You promised you would.

LORRAINE: *(to Ernie)* Oh, all right. I will.

ERNIE: You ready?

LORRAINE: Yeah.

ERNIE: No peeking.

LIFEGUARD: They're coming! They'll be here any moment now!

> *The Swimmers come sliding, crawling onto the beach.*
>
> *They're dripping wet and still wear the face masks and snorkels.*
>
> *Ernie lies on his back. Lorraine waits a moment, then lies beside him.*

They're here! Run while you can!

> *The Lifeguard blows his whistle.*

They're not ready yet. They don't understand.

> *The Man Swimmer stands behind Lorraine, the Woman Swimmer stands beside Ernie. The Lifeguard blows his whistle again.*

This is a public beach. Clear the beach. Come on, let's go.

LORRAINE: Are your eyes open?

ERNIE: Course they aren't.

LORRAINE: Just checking.

LIFEGUARD: Come on. We don't have all day.

> *The Man Swimmer takes hold of Lorraine's hand. The Woman Swimmer takes hold of Ernie's hand.*

ERNIE: I felt some drops of water.

LORRAINE: Probably just the ocean spray, Ernie.

ERNIE: Yeah. Probably.

> *The lights fade.*
>
> *The Lifeguard blows his whistle.*
>
> *Darkness.*

> *The End*

electric
gunfighters

CHARACTERS

PETE

BOB

Both are in their early twenties.
Each wears a holster and a gun.
Bob wears a cowboy hat. Pete doesn't.

A television is centred on the stage.
It's turned on but the screen contains no image.
Only interference.

ELECTRIC GUNFIGHTERS was first produced at Tarragon Theatre,
Toronto, in 1973, with the following cast:

BOB	Les Carlson
PETE	Steve Whistance-Smith

Directed by Candace O'Connor

ELECTRIC GUNFIGHTERS

As the lights come up, we see Pete lying on the floor, leaning against the left side of the TV. Bob lies on the floor on the right side of the TV.

PETE: You awake?

BOB: Yeah, I'm awake.

PETE: You hear that coyote last night?

BOB: I sure did. I thought he'd never stop howlin.

PETE: He must have been hungry.

BOB: Coyotes always are. As soon as they're done eatin, they're out lookin for more.

PETE: You reckon Billy left town?

BOB: Nope.

PETE: I bet Charlie's still there too.

Pete brings his legs up until his knees are under his chin.

BOB: I bet there's going to be trouble.

Pete turns and faces out.

Lots of trouble.

PETE: Thought I told you to be out of town before sunrise.

BOB: You sure did, sheriff.

PETE: Don't look like you went.

Pause. Pete crouches beside the TV now. Bob brings his legs up until his knees are under his chin and then he turns and faces out.

Folks in this town want to keep it nice and quiet. They don't want no gunslingers round here.

Pete stands.

BOB: I ain't no gunslinger.

PETE: You ain't no preacher neither.

BOB: I'm lookin for work.

PETE: What kind of work?

BOB: Ridin herd. Brandin. Checkin fences.

PETE: Mighty nice gun you got there. A Smith-Wesson?

BOB: A double-action Colt.

Pause. Bob stands.

So you don't know of any ranches hirin on?

PETE: Can't say that I do. Guess you'll just have to be movin on.

BOB: And if I don't?

PETE: I'll have to arrest you.

Pete moves out from the TV, facing Bob, ready to draw.

BOB: You can't arrest me.

PETE: Then I'll have to talk some sense into you.

BOB: Meanin what?

Pete gestures to his gun.

But I'd kill you.

Bob moves out from the TV and faces Pete.

I'm faster than you or any man in the territory.

Pete steps towards Bob.

You're all washed up, sheriff.

Bob steps towards Pete.

PETE: You ready?

BOB: Make your move.

PETE: Make yours.

They take another step closer.

They stare at each other, ready to draw.

BOB: What you waitin for, sheriff?

Pause.

PETE: For you.

Pause.

BOB: I ain't talkin no more.

Pause.

PETE: Me neither.

They both draw at the same time.

BOB: Kapow!

PETE: Kapow!

BOB: Kapow!

Pete is hit in his side and he walks towards Bob, who is still firing.

Kapow! Kapow! Kapow!

Bob catches him as he falls over and lowers him to the ground.

PETE: *(dying now)* I'm goin fast!

Bob kneels beside him.

BOB: I warned you.

PETE: I know.

BOB: I didn't want to fight you.

PETE: I know.

BOB: Where does it hurt?

> *Pete raises his arms straight up in the air.*

PETE: I'm goin fast! I'm goin fast! Jesus H. Christ, if you're comin for me, you'd better come quick!

> *Pete shakes his legs violently, still holding his arms up in the air and then he lies still. Bob puts his head on Pete's chest.*

BOB: Deader than a doornail.

> *Bob pushes down Pete's left arm, then his right arm. Satisfied with Pete's position, Bob stands and goes to the TV. Pete opens his eyes and watches Bob as he walks round the TV and then closes them as Bob comes back and stands beside him.*

BOB: Hello, Charlie.

PETE: How the hell are you, Billy!

BOB: It's good to lay eyes on you again.

PETE: It's been a long time, hasn't it?

BOB: I'll say.

> *Pete stands.*

PETE: Where you been?

BOB: Saskatchewan. Manitoba.

PETE: Good time?

BOB: Just driftin around. Where you been?

PETE: Out to the coast. British Columbia.

BOB: How was it?

PETE: Lot of nice saloons. Lot of money floatin around.

BOB: I hear they have some big trees out there.

PETE: Biggest I ever seen. Those Douglas Firs go straight up for hundreds of feet. Takes almost a day for two men to bring one down.

BOB: How's your shootin, Charlie?

PETE: The same as before.

BOB: Bet you can outshoot me.

PETE: Bet I can't.

BOB: You want to go first?

PETE: You go first.

Pete picks up a rock.

PETE: You ready?

Bob takes his gun out of its holster.

BOB: Let her go.

Pete throws the rock up in the air.

Kapow! Kapow! Kapow! Kapow!

Pete picks up the rock.

PETE: Three times.

BOB: Is that all?

PETE: That's good shootin, Billy.

BOB: Throw up another one.

Pete throws up another rock.

Kapow! Kapow! Kapow! Kapow!

Pete picks up the rock.

PETE: Perfect score.

BOB: Your turn now.

Pause. Bob picks up a rock.

Ready?

Pete takes out his gun. Bob throws the rock in the air. Pete aims his gun but doesn't fire.

Charlie. You didn't shoot.

PETE: I wasn't ready.

BOB: Let's try her again.

Bob picks up the rock and throws it.

PETE: Kapow! Kapow! Kapow! Kapow!

Bob picks up the rock.

BOB: You only hit it twice. That ain't like you at all.

Pete turns away from him and puts his gun back in the holster.

PETE: I know. But ever since Blazer's Mill I can't hit anything. I can't get Shotgun Roberts out of my head.

BOB: That no-good varmint!

PETE: I keep seein his ugly face. I keep seein me draw my gun. Squeezin the trigger. Him liftin his Winchester to his shoulder. Then my bullet's gone and I'm goin with it, like I was ridin a good horse cross open ground, and that bullet keeps on goin and we're almost there when he squeezes his trigger and his bullet goes past but we know it's too late for Shotgun and we smash through his skin right into the stomach!

Pete is shot in the stomach and grabs himself with his hands.

BOB: Charlie!

PETE: There's blood and guts all over us and we're slowin down but we know we really got him good. It may take a while but we really . . . and he's fallin . . .

> *Pete falls down on his knees, still holding his stomach, then he falls over onto his side.*

. . . smashin into the ground and everything twists around again and there's more blood and he's pissin in his pants and we're not movin anymore, not movin anywhere . . .

BOB: Charlie! Wake up!

PETE: I saw his bullet comin, so I dropped and kept on rollin and firin.

BOB: *(shaking him)* Wake up!

PETE: His bullet missed me by a mile.

BOB: *(shaking him)* That was over a year ago.

PETE: *(sitting up)* Stop it! Stop shakin me, Billy!

BOB: You okay?

PETE: Yeah. I'm okay.

BOB: You sure?

PETE: Yeah, I'm sure.

> *Pause. Bob walks downstage from Pete. He lifts his hat, wipes his forehead with the sleeve of his shirt, puts the hat on his head.*

BOB: This looks bad.

PETE: What does?

BOB: This wagon train. They must have hit em just at dawn.

> *Pause. Bob bends over to have a closer look at the dead woman.*

All of em are still layin in the wagons except for this dead woman.

> *Pause. Pete stands, joins Bob.*

There ain't a bit of clothin left on her.

PETE: She's a fine lookin woman.

BOB: She's nice all right.

PETE: She must have been some woman with that brown hair.

BOB: Those eyes.

PETE: That face.

BOB: Those breasts.

> *Pete kneels beside Bob, pokes the dead woman in the side with his finger.*

PETE: She's a bit soft.

BOB: A sheepherder came across a burnt-out wagon train this side of the Snake River. He moseyed around the smokin wagons, just in case there was anything valuable and then he came across this dead woman lyin in the grass.

PETE: I've heard it before.

BOB: Now this sheepherder had been out on the prairie a long time.

PETE: *(standing)* We ought to bury her.

BOB: It was almost a year since he'd been in any kind of town and almost two months since he talked to something besides sheep.

PETE: I said we should bury her!

BOB: I heard you! But if we bury her then we have to bury em all. And that's a hell of a lot of work when there's coyotes around.

PETE: I still think we should.

BOB: After a couple of nights this place would be cleaned right up, cause once they pick up the scent they won't leave it alone.

Pause. Bob walks away from him.

PETE: Billy.

BOB: What is it now?

Pete draws his gun.

PETE: *(whisper)* I heard something.

BOB: You're always hearin things.

PETE: *(whisper)* I swear I did.

Pause. Pete crosses to him.

(whisper) A twig snapped.

BOB: Where?

PETE: *(whisper — pointing)* Over there.

BOB: I don't see nothin.

PETE: What's the matter with you?

BOB: Get down!

Bob lies on the ground. Pete scrambles down beside him.

PETE: So I didn't hear anything, eh?

BOB: I think I've spotted one on your left!

PETE: You got him lined up?

BOB: Yeah. There's another one now.

They both have drawn their guns.

Kablammo!

PETE: Kapow! Kapow!

BOB: Kablammo!

PETE: Kapow! Kapow!

BOB: Kablammo!

PETE: Kapow! Kapow!

BOB: They're runnin, Charlie!

PETE: Kapow! Kapow!

BOB: Look at em go!

PETE: We licked em! We won!

BOB: We slaughtered em!

PETE: We showed em!

BOB: We massacred em!

> *They put their guns back in their holsters.*

They can run when they want to.

> *Bob crosses to the TV and sits in front of it.*

PETE: They sure can.

BOB: Shucks, I'm all tuckered out.

> *Bob fans himself with his hat.*
>
> *Pete leans on the TV.*

PETE: Same here.

> *Pause.*

BOB: Poor old sheepherder.

PETE: What's that?

BOB: Almost two months since he talked to something besides sheep.

PETE: I've heard it, Billy!

> *Pause. Pete walks away from the TV.*

BOB: I don't see you tellin me no yarns.

PETE: At least I don't tell the same ones.

BOB: Have to pass the time, don't we?

> *Pause. Pete takes out his harmonica, puts it to his mouth, then lowers it again.*

PETE: Billy.

BOB: Yeah, Charlie.

PETE: What if some cowboy asked you how come you're always Billy and I'm always Charlie?

BOB: How come he'd ask such a fool question?

PETE: I don't know. What if he did?

BOB: Well now. I'd tell him like it is. I was born Billy and you was born Charlie.

PETE: But what if he asked why I couldn't be Billy?

BOB: What would he do that for? I'm me and you're you and I ride with you cause there ain't no one else as good as you are.

PETE: That's what you'd tell him?

BOB: No one can ride or shoot like you.

PETE: You're faster.

BOB: Maybe.

PETE: You are and you know it.

BOB: It ain't by much.

PETE: It was by quite a bit today.

BOB: It happens to the best, Charlie. I've seen real mean gunfighters, who've killed twenty men, freeze up. That happens cause they don't work on their delivery. A smooth draw is what you need to stay alive around here. You may be fast but sooner or later you'll run across someone who's as fast as you are. *(Bob stands)* The gunfighter who has a delivery never freezes up. He works on it every minute of the day. It's part of the way he walks, wears his hat, drinks his whisky. Your delivery should be as natural as ridin a horse. Either you ride with it or else you fight it, like a city slicker bouncin up and down on the horse's back.

Bob steps out from the TV in a gunfighter's stance.

Cause when you're standin in the street with the dust and horseshit and flies buzzin around and the sun beatin down on you and Slim Jackson is about thirty feet from you and he's as fast as a rattler and he's already killed fifteen men and then you start movin for him. And you know everyone in this stinkin town stuck out on the prairie is watchin and they don't give a damn just as long as you get it over with and now Slim's only twenty feet away and you can see patches of sweat under his arms but you can't see his eyes cause they're shaded by his hat and you're thinkin when? When will he make his move? Now? Is it now? And Slim keeps comin closer and a dog starts barking and then another dog is barking too . . .

PETE: Billy!

BOB: And he's gettin closer.

PETE: *(shaking him)* Wake up!

BOB: He's goin to draw any moment now.

PETE: *(shaking him)* Billy!

BOB: What are you shakin me for?

PETE: You okay?

BOB: Yeah.

PETE: You sure? Cause the posse's comin.

BOB: Is there many?

PETE: At least twenty men. Maybe more.

> *They both draw their guns and back up slowly towards the TV.*

You shouldn't have killed that clerk at the bank.

BOB: He was in the way.

PETE: He got scared, that's all.

BOB: I don't like knockin people off.

PETE: Then why'd you do it?

BOB: It was either him or you and I figure you ride a hell of a lot better than him.

PETE: Much obliged.

BOB: Don't mention it.

PETE: I'll take the right.

BOB: Guess that leaves me with the left. Here they come. Kablammo!

PETE: Kapow! Kapow!

BOB: Kablammo!

PETE: Kapow! Kapow!

BOB: Kablammo!

> *Pete is hit in the chest this time. He falls out in front of the TV.*

How bad is it, Charlie?

PETE: Real bad.

BOB: Don't worry, you'll pull through. Kablammo!

PETE: I ain't goin to.

BOB: Kablammo! Kablammo!

PETE: Billy, I ain't goin to make it.

BOB: Sure you are. Can you hold out till nightfall?

PETE: Hell no! Give me a gun and I'll cover you while you get away.

BOB: I ain't leavin you here.

PETE: I'm not goin anywhere, except six feet under.

BOB: I'll get you out of here. Kablammo! Kablammo!

PETE: Give me a gun!

BOB: Kablammo! Kablammo!

PETE: Listen to me.

BOB: Kablammo! Kablammo!

PETE: GIVE ME A GUN, BILLY!

BOB: So you can get shot up again? Hell no! Everytime there's a gunfight you get shot and die. You ain't havin no gun this time. You're goin to stay there till we can make a break. Kablammo! Kablammo! Every time. Every time you do this. Kablammo! *(Pete sits up)* Get down! You'll get shot!

PETE:	BOB:
We were in the living room, watching television, when Bob went over to the set and stuck his arm through the screen up to his elbow. Then he pulled it back out and grinned at us. Nothing was wrong with his arm or the screen. The Lone Ranger and Tonto were still chasing outlaws in the hills. And then Bob dared us to do the same thing but we said it was some kind of trick. We never thought Brylcream would do it cause he's such a dope and he has these boils on his neck and greasy black hair and he always watches TV with us even though he knows we don't want him there. So Brylcream puts his arm through the screen and it doesn't break and the Lone Ranger and Tonto are galloping around his arm and we're whistling and clapping for Brylcream and maybe this made him excited because his arm went in the screen to his shoulder, then his head was going inside and before any of us moved he was up to his waist in the set. Bob and I grabbed his legs. We pulled as hard as we could but it was like he was sucked in there by a huge vacuum cleaner. And the opening in the screen got bigger and bigger, like a mouth, and soon Brylcream was up to his thighs and sliding in even faster and then we couldn't hold him any longer and the screen swallowed him up and then it closed. The screen was solid, nothing was scratched. We looked but Brylcream wasn't with the Lone Ranger and Tonto. We changed every channel but he wasn't there. He wasn't anywhere.	Get down! You'll get killed! *(Pete stands. He moves out from the TV, much as Bob did earlier. Bob puts his gun in his holster and stands in front of the TV)* You'll never get away with it, Charlie. I've rode with you a long time and this is just another of your tall tales. Now, I wouldn't mind so much, if there was truth to em. You can tell em to your saloon women but you're wastin your breath with me. You don't have to go through all this rigmarole if you want something. Just come out and say what you want. *(pause)* And then we can do something about it, Pete. All you have to do is turn it. How about channel one? *(Bob changes the channel on the TV. It still has interference)* That's where Billy kills his first man. *(turning channel)* Channel two? Billy meets his girlfriend for the first time. *(turning channel)* Channel three? Billy and Charlie come across a burnt-out wagon train. *(turning channel)* They rustle some horses. *(turning channel)* Billy saves Charlie's life for the second time. *(turning channel)* Channel seven? Billy has a showdown with the sheriff. *(turning channel)* Channel eight? They rob a train. *(turning each time)* Channel nine? Channel ten? Channel twelve? Thirteen? Fourteen? Fifteen? Sixteen? Seventeen? Channel twenty-five? Channel thirty-nine? *(Bob stops changing channels and looks at Pete, who stands fifteen feet from the TV and facing the audience)*

Pause.

BOB: You all right?

PETE: Same as always.

BOB: You find anything?

PETE: Like what?

BOB: Anything different?

PETE: Just two cowboys.

BOB: Anyone we know?

PETE: Can't really tell cause their faces are messed up real bad, Slim.
Looks like they were ripped apart by teeth.

BOB: You want to bury 'em, Shotgun?

PETE: They can wait till mornin. I reckon it's time we turned in.

BOB: Yeah.

> *Pause. Pete comes back to the TV and crouches down on the
> right side. Bob crouches on the other side.*

PETE: You built a nice campfire, Slim.

> *He warms his hands at the fire.*

BOB: You need one when you're out on the prairie.

PETE: Yeah.

BOB: In case something tries to get too close. *(Pause)* A sheepherder came
across a burnt-out wagon train next to the Snake River. He moseyed around
and found this dead woman. It was three months since he talked to something
besides sheep. He looked around. No one except her dead ma and pa. Nothin
except miles and miles of open prairie. So he . . .

> *Pause.*

PETE: What?

BOB: I don't know. I forget how it ends.

PETE: You couldn't have.

BOB: Do you know the story?

PETE: You were the one tellin it!

BOB: I know.

> *Pause.*

PETE: Just look at all them stars.

BOB: Yeah. There must be millions.

PETE: It sure would take a long time to count them.

> *Pause. Pete takes out his harmonica.*

BOB: Well. I guess I'll get me some shuteye.

PETE: Me too.

BOB: Night.

PETE: Sleep well.

> *Pete plays softly on his harmonica. Both remain crouching beside the TV as the lights fade.*

> *The End*

blitzkrieg

To Eric Steiner, a great director.

CHARACTERS

ADOLF HITLER	He is in his fifties, he wears his military uniform with the black boots.
EVA BRAUN	His mistress, thirty-one, who dresses in the most exclusive way the Forties can offer.
MARTIN BORMANN	Hitler's personal secretary, who is in his forties.
GRETL BRAUN	Eva's younger sister, who is in her late twenties.

All the action takes place in Eva's salon at the Berghof, Hitler's chalet in the Bavarian Alps.

BLITZKRIEG was first produced by Tarragon Theatre at the Poor Alex Theatre, Toronto, in February 1974 with the following cast:

HITLER	George Dawson
EVA	Brenda Donohue
GRETL	Fiona Reid
BORMANN	Don MacQuarrie

Directed by Eric Steiner
Designed by Marti Wright

BLITZKRIEG

Scene One

Afternoon. The sun coming through windows. Birds singing. Adolf sits in an easy chair, drinking tea. Eva sits on the sofa with her tea. Obviously they have just come from lunch.

ADOLF: So you had sweet dreams last night?

EVA: I always do after *Grand Hotel.*

ADOLF: I'm glad you enjoyed it.

EVA: I loved it.

ADOLF: How many times is that now?

EVA: Five. I've seen it five times all together.

ADOLF: And you still enjoy it?

EVA: It's better every time I see it. It's one of the best movies ever made.

>*Eva puts her tea-cup down and stands. She walks, with all the self-confidence of a professional model, over to Adolf. Then she kisses him on the top of his head.*

ADOLF: What was that for?

EVA: I was thanking you.

ADOLF: Don't be ridiculous, Eva.

>*Adolf holds out his tea-cup.*

I'd like some more.

>*Eva takes it and walks back to get her cup. Adolf watches her walk.*

What are you walking like that for?

EVA: *(turning around, facing him)* I thought you liked it.

ADOLF: I do, but there's no need to flaunt it.

>*Eva walks past him with both cups to the serving table.*

Is there?

EVA: I always say, when you have it you should flaunt it.

>*She pours tea into the two cups.*

ADOLF: Watch where you do flaunt it in the future.

EVA: Worried?

ADOLF: There's a lot of rats around these days.

Eva pours milk into the two cups.

EVA: Meaning?

ADOLF: Hungry rats don't nibble when they smell cheese. They gobble up the whole piece.

Eva walks back and hands Adolf his cup of tea.

EVA: I know one when I see one.

ADOLF: They come in a lot of disguises these days. It doesn't pay to trust anyone because they might turn out to be a rat.

Eva sits on the sofa.

You understand?

EVA: I understand.

Pause. Eva looks at Adolf as she stirs her tea.

It's too bad you had to leave in the middle of the movie.

ADOLF: It was a phone call from Berlin.

EVA: Serious?

ADOLF: Not really. It was just a report.

EVA: You were gone long enough.

ADOLF: It was a long report.

EVA: It must have been.

Pause. Eva looks at Adolf as she sips her tea.

You missed the best part of the movie. The part where Greta Garbo comes back to the Grand Hotel after she's danced to a half-empty theatre and she's depressed.

ADOLF: She's a singer, isn't she?

EVA: No, she's a famous ballerina.

ADOLF: I always thought she was a singer.

EVA: You know she's a dancer, you've seen the movie with me enough times. Anyway, she's very depressed and so she dismisses her manager and maid.

ADOLF: What's she so depressed about?

EVA: Because nothing seems to be going right in her life. So she takes out her gun and —

ADOLF: What's she going to do with that?

EVA: She's going to kill herself.

ADOLF: What for?

EVA: Because she sees no other way out.

ADOLF: But she doesn't manage to kill herself.

EVA: No, because John Barrymore steps out from behind the curtain.

ADOLF: And she shoots him?

EVA: You know that she doesn't.

ADOLF: I'd shoot someone if he was hiding behind my curtains.

EVA: You would do something like that.

ADOLF: It's simple, shoot first and ask the questions later.

EVA: May I get back to the movie?

ADOLF: Continue by all means.

EVA: All right. He takes the gun away and then she tries to throw him out but he tells her how he's loved her since the first time he saw her and how he figured the only way he could meet her was to sneak into her room.

ADOLF: And she believes him.

EVA: She only has to look in his eyes to know that he's telling the truth.

ADOLF: But he'd already stolen her pearl necklace.

EVA: That's what is so beautiful about it, because we know that and he knows that but she doesn't. And they talk together all night and they fall in love. He even falls more in love with her.

ADOLF: She's a fool.

EVA: She's a woman.

ADOLF: She should have kicked him out.

EVA: But he tells her about the necklace in the morning and she forgives him.

ADOLF: She's even a bigger fool when she does that.'

EVA: No, she's not. He's been honest with her and that's the only way love can survive in the world.

ADOLF: You can't be honest with people. They'll slit your throat as soon as you've finished shaking hands if it will help them. Look at the Jews. They'd sell their own mother if it would help them.

EVA: Please, no politics this afternoon.

ADOLF: All right, Effie.

EVA: So they plan to run away to Italy and live in her villa for the rest of their lives.

ADOLF: And he gets killed.

EVA: But that's because he's too proud to admit to her that he doesn't have enough money for the train fare and so he tries to rob someone else and there's a fight and he's killed.

ADOLF: You mean, he doesn't survive.

EVA: No, that's not the point. That's not it at all. The real tragedy is that Greta doesn't know he's dead and everyone at the hotel knows it but they won't tell her. Every time I see the movie I want to warn her. Because she's so happy while she packs all her suitcases and trunks, she's singing and dancing around the room. And she's happy when she goes downstairs to the lobby. And she's happy when she gets into the taxi. And that's the end of the movie. But can you imagine her waiting for him at the train station because he promised to meet her there and then the whistle blows and she has to climb aboard and then as the train pulls out of the station, she must be looking out the window, searching the platform. And you always wonder whether she'll go through the rest of her life thinking he didn't love her at all. Or whether she'll find out the truth, that he really did love her.

Eva gets up with her cup in her hand and walks to the window. Adolf watches her.

ADOLF: It's a very touching story but you should remember, Eva, that it's a movie.

EVA: I know that.

ADOLF: You should also remember they're actors saying their lines. They're posing as people who don't really exist.

EVA: I know that too.

ADOLF: There's no place for their kind of love in the world now. No place at all for it.

Eva lifts the cup high above her head and smashes it on the floor. Hold. Eva standing at the window, Adolf in his chair, watching her. Then blackout.

Scene Two

Eva sits in the easy chair. She is painting her nails with red nail polish and after she finishes each nail, she watches Adolf as he walks up and down in front of her.

When Adolf isn't gesturing with his hands, he keeps them folded over each other, covering his groin. He walks as if he were a sentry on duty, walking ten feet and then turning around to walk back again.

ADOLF: It's always quiet the night after a big attack and the enemy had attacked that day with everything they had. They started shelling about four a.m. and at six the first wave of men came out of the trenches. They sent thousands and thousands of men but they didn't gain an inch. Our machine guns cut them down in no man's land. Some were still alive because we could hear them moaning in the dark, asking for help. And every time the breeze changed direction you could smell the stench from the corpses.

Adolf stops walking.

Suddenly there was this squeaking noise. And the biggest rat I'd ever seen, scurried past me down the trench. Then two more rats ran past me. But rats are nothing in the trenches. After a while it's as if they're fighting with you. You eat with them at your feet, you sleep with them running all over you, you shoot at them in no man's land. But all this time the squeaking noise kept getting louder, so I looked and coming towards me were rats. Thousands and thousands of rats, which had eyes that glowed in the dark.

Adolf walks back and forth again.

You can imagine what it's like running across no man's land in the dark. I kept falling across dead bodies and into shell holes and I kept getting up and running again and all the time they were getting closer and their red eyes were getting bigger and bigger. Then I was caught in the barbed wire. I tried to pull myself free but the more I twisted on the ground the deeper the barbs dug into me. By this time the rats had surrounded me. They didn't bite me, they just sniffed at my legs and squeaked to each other in their rat talk. I kept looking at them, watching them with my eyes, especially the rat that was between my legs. He was bigger and he seemed to have some kind of control over the thousands of rats around us. We watched each other. I made sure he looked into my eyes, deep into them, and then we made contact. My mind locked into his and his mind was locked into the minds of all the rats. I thought about him jumping off the ground three feet. He jumped three feet. I thought about him making a somersault in the air. He jumped and made a somersault. All their minds were open to me and waiting for an order. I thought about them running to the shell hole twenty feet behind me. Immediately they started running and squeaking and trampling each other to get to the shell hole. The rats who got there first ate the uniforms off the dead men and soon they were chewing away at their stomachs and faces. After that you couldn't see anything except more and more rats and it looked like a small mountain of moving rats, turning and twisting to get at the men. The blood must have excited them because they started fighting and biting and ripping huge gashes in each other, and snapping off tails and chewing on the heads of dead rats and blood was spurting everywhere and the noise was incredible because they were all squeaking as loud as they could and their teeth were constantly scraping against bones, which sent chills up and down my spine. I tried to stop them. I tried to make them come back. But I couldn't. They were all blocked, completely blocked.

Pause. Eva holds up her right hand and blows on her nails to dry them.

EVA: So that was it.

ADOLF: Yes, that was it.

EVA: That's when you woke up?

ADOLF: That was the end of my dream.

EVA: I'm glad I don't have ones like that.

ADOLF: I hate it when you wake up before you've finished. I didn't get to see whether the rats stayed in the shell hole.

Adolf sits down on the sofa.

EVA: I hate it when chills run up and down my spine.

ADOLF: So do I.

EVA: When that happens, you're supposed to have a tragic death.

ADOLF: Who says so?

EVA: It was a story my mother used to tell me when I was very young.

ADOLF: I don't believe any of those folk-tales.

EVA: I don't either, but some people believe in them.

ADOLF: Some people will believe anything.

> *Pause. Eva puts the top back on the nail polish bottle. Then she stands and goes to Adolf.*

EVA: How do you like my nails? They're quite long now.

> *She shows him her nails.*

ADOLF: Yes, they're quite nice.

EVA: They're a lot sharper too. Feel them.

> *Eva runs her nails lightly across Adolf's face.*

They're pretty nice, aren't they?

ADOLF: Yes, they are.

> *You can hear the sound of planes in the distance; the sound gradually becomes louder.*

What's that?

EVA: What's what?

ADOLF: Don't you hear it?

EVA: No, I don't hear anything.

ADOLF: Listen

> *Adolf stands.*

EVA: Planes.

ADOLF: Sounds like a lot of them.

EVA: Sounds like bombers.

ADOLF: Don't be ridiculous, you can't tell what they are this far away.

EVA: They sounded the same when I was in Munich and they almost destroyed the city that time.

ADOLF: It doesn't have to be their planes, they could be ours. They could be coming back from a mission.

EVA: They could be coming on one too.

ADOLF: I refuse to believe it.

EVA: I don't want to believe it either.

ADOLF: I refuse, I absolutely refuse to believe it. Do you understand? Where's Bormann? He'll know whether they're our planes or not.

Adolf goes to the door and opens it.

I want Bormann and I want him right now! Not tomorrow or next week! I want him right now!

Adolph slams the door shut and comes back to the middle of the room.

EVA: And what if he doesn't know?

ADOLF: Bormann always knows. It's his duty to know everything and he'll know what they are. But don't worry, Eva, what you saw in Munich that day will never happen again. Never in a thousand years. Because the scientists of the Reich have been working day and night on a weapon so powerful and capable of total destruction that it will make our bombing of London seem like child's play.

Adolf says the next section of his monologue to the ceiling, as if he believed the pilots could hear him. Martin comes into the room halfway through Adolf's monologue. He stands by the door. Adolf doesn't notice him at all.

It will be our new blitzkrieg. In a matter of seconds it will flatten cities, it will kill millions of people, it will injure millions more, it will lay waste to the countryside. All this in a few seconds of brilliant flashing light, a thousand times brighter than the sun. We will no longer need hundreds of planes or armies to strike like we did in Poland or France or Russia. Because our new weapon is like the lightning itself. It can destroy instantly. Do you understand? It can destroy instantly whatever and wherever it wants. All we will need is a few planes equipped with the new weapon and the decision from me. Because I decide what city will survive and what city will be destroyed.

The planes are closer now, so it's harder to hear Adolf.

I decide with a simple yes or no whether millions will live or die. I am the one who decides. Do you understand? I am the one who controls the blitzkrieg! I am the one who tells it what to do! I am the blitzkrieg! No one else controls it! No one in the whole world!

Adolf shakes his fists at the planes, which sound deafening now. Eva, bored, looks up at the ceiling. Martin still stands by the door. Hold. Perhaps for ten seconds or longer, until the sound of the planes recedes. Martin takes a step forward.

MARTIN: You wanted me, my Fuhrer.

ADOLF: *(turning on him, coldly furious)* And what took you so long?

MARTIN: I came as soon as I could. I was reading some reports.

ADOLF: I will tolerate no excuses for you taking so long. When I call you, I expect you here immediately. Do you understand?

MARTIN: Perfectly. I apologize for my delay.

ADOLF: Who do those planes belong to?

MARTIN: I assume they must be ours. If no alarm was given —

ADOLF: You assume! Don't you know?

MARTIN: It's only logical they are because they would have never been allowed this close.

ADOLF: But you don't know, do you?

MARTIN: I can find out easily enough.

ADOLF: Let's both go and find out.

MARTIN: That isn't necessary. I can have all the information back to you before —

> Adolf leaves before he's finished. Martin looks at Eva, who shrugs her shoulders, and then he follows his leader out the door. Eva wanders around the room, picking up things, putting them down again, out of the nervous habit of having to do something.

EVA: I don't know how he can stand it sometimes. Everywhere the Chief goes, he has to go. Everywhere the Chief is, Martin Bormann has to be there too. He must never have a minute to himself, never a moment's rest.

> Eva stops in front of the cabinet, opens the top drawer and looks inside it. She's reaching inside the drawer when Gretl comes into the room, knocking on the door as she does.

GRETL: Anyone home?

EVA: I am.

> Eva slides the drawer shut.

GRETL: I came to see if you want to go for a walk down to the village. It's a beautiful day outside. The sky doesn't have a cloud in it, not one.

EVA: I don't know, Gretl. I'd like to.

GRETL: Come on. You haven't been outside for a week now. You'll be forgetting how to walk soon.

EVA: I don't think I better. The Chief might need me for something.

GRETL: He won't miss you for an hour.

EVA: You know, he hasn't been at his best lately.

GRETL: He looks fine to me.

EVA: I'd better wait and ask him if it's all right to go.

GRETL: Well, I'm not waiting around all day.

EVA: You won't have to. He'll be right back.

GRETL: Two days ago we were supposed to go hiking up in the mountains but he never came back. He was gone for hours.

EVA: That meeting wasn't his fault.

GRETL: I didn't say it was. Well. I guess I better go now if I want some sunshine today.

She turns to leave.

EVA: Wait a minute.

GRETL: What is it?

EVA: *(hesitant)* No, you better go by yourself. I'll go with you tomorrow.

GRETL: I'll believe that when it happens. I'll see you later.

> *Gretl leaves. Eva takes a cigarette pack out of her bag, takes out a cigarette, puts the pack in the bag. She looks at her wristwatch and then sits on the sofa. She lights the cigarette and holds the match in front of her, watching it. Hold. She blows out the match. Then blackout.*

Scene Three

> *Soon it will be dusk. The smashed china hasn't been cleaned up and the floor is littered with paper airplanes.*
>
> *Adolf sits on the sofa reading a report. He wears reading glasses. There is a small pile of reports beside him on the sofa.*
>
> *Eva sits on the rug in front of Adolf. She has some sheets of paper in front of her. She is folding one sheet in half, to make another paper airplane*

EVA: I'll be glad when this is all over and we can do what we want to do. It all gets so boring. The same people saying the same things day after day. I think it would be so nice to go somewhere.

> *Pause. Adolf keeps reading; Eva keeps folding the piece of paper.*

It would be nice to go somewhere, wouldn't it?

ADOLF: *(without looking up)* It certainly would.

EVA: My trip to Italy seems like such a long time ago. I guess three months isn't that long but it seems like three years now. Of course, travelling with your mother and your sister isn't very exciting. I would have rather gone with you, like we did when you visited Mussolini. There's something about the sun in Italy. It's always so bright down there. You know, living in the Berghof is so beautiful, what with the mountains and all the meadows to go walking in, but I still have this feeling sometimes, where it all seems like a dream. Sometimes it gets so bad I think someone will come along and pinch me and I'll wake up and you'll be gone and I'll be back home with my father and mother and Gretl and everything will be gone. What do you think of that?

ADOLF: *(without looking up)* That's very interesting.

Eva holds up the finished airplane and throws it at Adolf, but it misses him and sails behind the sofa. Adolf keeps reading his report.

EVA: We're still going to Hollywood after this is over, aren't we? You promised that we could make the movie in California, where the sun shines all the time and where you can walk down any street and run into a movie star.

Eva takes another sheet of paper and folds it in half.

It's only fair the rest of the world knows how we met. They deserve to see how beautiful it was. I think it would be exciting to act in a movie about yourself. Don't you think so? I think it would be.

ADOLF: *(still not looking up)* Of course it would.

EVA: It was at Hoffman's photography studio where we met. I was standing on the ladder, trying to reach something on the top shelf when I heard you come into the shop. I knew you were staring at my legs but what could I say? I couldn't tell you to stop looking. But then I liked it too, because it felt like you were running your hands up and down my legs with your eyes. And after I climbed down, Hoffman asked me over to the table where you were sitting and asked me if I would get some beer and sausage from the corner tavern. And like a fool, I went. I was only seventeen. I didn't know that was his way of saying sit down and make yourself comfortable. And when I came back you ate the sausage and you don't even eat meat. You must have been impressed with my legs, eh?

Eva throws the airplane at Adolf and hits him on the chest.

Bullseye!

Adolf looks at her and then crumples the airplane in his hand.

ADOLF: Effie, you are not only making a mess but you are being a nuisance. I will not tolerate it much longer. Do you understand?

EVA: Yes, but I don't see why you have to read all those boring reports now.

ADOLF: There's an important meeting tonight.

EVA: *(sulking)* There's one every night.

ADOLF: Don't worry, I'll make it as short as possible. My generals are not the most pleasant company. I prefer to spend my time with you but now I have to read these reports. My generals would love it if I wasn't prepared.

Adolf goes back to his reading. Eva stands, picks up a paper airplane off the floor and makes a few passes through the air with it. Then she walks behind Adolf and makes a sweep with the airplane past Adolf's head.

EVA: ZOOOOOOOOOOMMMMMMMM! You could have been strafed right then. You could be full of bullet holes now, writhing on the floor, blood pouring out of you.

Eva makes another pass at his head.

ZOOOOOOMMMMMMM! This time it's a bomber coming in low dropping its bombs on top of your head. Dropping tons and tons of bombs on you. You would be blasted to a million trillion pieces and they'd never be able to find all the pieces. Never in a thousand years. ZOOOOOOOOOMMMMMM! ZOOOOOOOOOOOOOMMMMMMMMMMMM!

> *Eva makes another pass with the airplane but this time Adolf grabs the airplane and crumples it in his hand.*

ADOLF: If you want to play, go outside and do it.

> *Eva moves away from him and picks up another plane. She keeps making passes in the air with it. Adolf ignores her and keeps reading.*

EVA: ZOOOOOOOMMMMMMM!   ZOOOOOooooooMMMMMMMMMM! zooooooooooOOOOOOOOOMMMMMMMMMM! Pilot to co-pilot, I've spotted our target in the field below. I think he's spotted us. Look at him running, trying to hide. He's a fool. He can't escape us, once we have him in our sights. Let's dive.

> *Eva dives with her airplane.*

zooooooooooOOOOOOOOOMMMMMMMMMM!

> *Eva mimes a machine gun.*

Rat-a-tat-tat-tat-tat-tat-tat-tat-tat-tat-tat-tat!

> *Eva levels off with her airplane.*

Pilot to co-pilot. I think we have ourselves a kill. Repeat. We have ourselves a kill. Let's clear out now. He won't be going anywhere for a long time.

> *Eva slides off with her airplane.*

ZOOOOOOOOOoooooooooommmmmmmmm! Pilot to co-pilot. He doesn't look like much from way up here, does he? Looks more like a rat to me. But let's go, it's time to head home.

> *Eva moves back to the table with her airplane.*

zooooooooOOOOOOOMMMMMMMMMMMMmmmmmmmmmmmmmmmm!

> *Eva lands the plane on the table.*

ADOLF: I hope you're finished with your little game now.

EVA: Don't worry, the mission's over. The pilot and co-pilot are in a tavern now, drinking schnapps.

ADOLF: Very funny, Eva.

EVA: It was a little strafing, that's all.

> *Eva sits beside him on the sofa.*

All in a day's work.

ADOLF: *(tapping the report)* And so is this.

> *Eva moves closer to him.*

EVA: Can I tell you something?

ADOLF: That depends on what it is.

Eva moves even closer to Adolf and puts her hand on his arm.

EVA: The day after we met I spent my whole lunch hour going through all your photographs at the studio. In one you would be making a speech, in another you would be shaking a hand, in another women would be trying to kiss you. Or they would be throwing flowers, or crying because you touched them. You looked so magnificent striding down the street in your uniform and your black boots, soldiers marching behind you, holding flags, cheering you on. But you know what I noticed?

Eva begins to play with his hair.

ADOLF: What.

EVA: What I really liked was your eyes. In every photograph, no matter what angle it was taken from, your eyes looked like they were from some other world. I felt them penetrating me.

Adolf gently lifts her hand away.

ADOLF: I really should be getting back to this.

EVA: You know how hard it is for me to control myself when you're around.

ADOLF: You promised me you'd be good this afternoon.

EVA: I could tell you were a strong man, one who would stop at nothing to get what he wanted. So many men are weaklings. They're afraid of themselves and their potential. So many of them are afraid to take a stand on anything. Women detest that kind of man. Women need strong men to tell them what to do.

ADOLF: They certainly do need that.

EVA: But men need women too. They need beautiful women who know how to please them, how to satisfy them. You can tell what a man likes the first time you meet him. I knew the first time I looked at you.

Eva stands.

ADOLF: Knew what?

EVA: What you liked.

Eva stands in front of Adolf and undoes the top button of her blouse.

ADOLF: Eva, not here.

EVA: Don't worry, the door's locked.

ADOLF: Not now.

EVA: The servants have instructions not to bother us.

ADOLF: There could be a phone call.

EVA: You can ignore it.

Eva undoes another button.

ADOLF: I'll leave if you keep this up.

EVA: No, you won't.

ADOLF: I will.

EVA: You won't leave because you like it too much. You know how you like watching me undo button by button . . . by button . . . by button . . .

Eva's blouse is undone now.

You know how you like me to stand close to you while I undress so you can smell my perfume. Smell it? It's Chanel today. It's nice, isn't it? And now we'll take off our blouse nice and slowly.

Eva takes off her blouse.

That's a lot better now, isn't it? And now we'll take off our skirt.

Eva slides her skirt down her legs. She's wearing a half-slip underneath it.

It's nice when we take our time like this. That's what is really exciting. It's the most exciting thing we've ever seen, isn't it? It most certainly is.

Eva steps out of her skirt.

And we have an erection already. We have an absolutely huge erection. One of the biggest ones we've ever had in our whole life. We certainly know how to have big ones. Come on, stand up. We can't sit there all day.

Eva takes Adolf's hands as he stands. She has hypnotized him with her body.

My, my, my. We have such a huge one today. We must have the biggest one the world has ever seen.

Adolf tries to embrace her but she moves out of reach. Red light from the sunset is gradually filling the room.

Now we mustn't do something like that. It's not very nice to rush things, is it?

ADOLF: No, it isn't.

EVA: Do we feel like dancing?

ADOLF: Yes, let's dance.

EVA: Do we really feel like it?

ADOLF: We do.

EVA: But are we sure we should dance right now?

ADOLF: Yes, we are.

EVA: Maybe we're too busy.

ADOLF: We aren't.

EVA: And we are so excited right now.

ADOLF: Yes, we are.

Adolf tries to embrace her again but she moves away.

EVA: Now, we mustn't get too close.

ADOLF: I'm sorry.

EVA: We're going to dance this one nice and slow.

ADOLF: Really nice and slow.

EVA: As slow as we can.

ADOLF: Yes.

EVA: Because we don't like fast numbers.

ADOLF: No, we hate them.

EVA: We never have liked fast ones.

> *Adolf shakes his head.*

Maybe we should get down on our knees first!

> *Adolf gets down on his knees.*

We like it down on the floor, don't we? Because down there we can see our legs much better.

> *Eva puts her shoe in the middle of Adolf's back and digs in her heel, forcing him to kneel lower.*

Do we want to touch our legs?

ADOLF: Yes, we'd like to.

EVA: They're so beautiful, aren't they?

ADOLF: Very beautiful.

EVA: So long and smooth to touch.

ADOLF: Very smooth.

EVA: So exciting to touch with our hands.

ADOLF: Very exciting.

EVA: And we like to be excited, don't we?

ADOLF: We love it.

> *Eva takes her foot off his back.*

EVA: Because when we're really excited, then we really love each other.

ADOLF: Yes, that's when we really love.

EVA: But first we want to look at the beautiful sunset.

> *Adolf moves as if to stand.*

We mustn't move. We wouldn't want to spoil all the excitement by moving, would we?

ADOLF: No, we wouldn't.

> *Eva moves to the window. The red light from the sunset is a brilliant red now. Adolf is still kneeling, with his arms stretched out in front of him.*

EVA: We're enjoying this, aren't we?

ADOLF: Yes, we are.

EVA: Because we never have seen such a beautiful sunset.

ADOLF: We never have.

EVA: And we know the sun is the most beautiful and the most dangerous thing in the sky. It gives us warmth and brilliant light day after day and yet if we look at it long enough, if we let its radioactive light into our eyes, it will blind us.

ADOLF: Blind us.

EVA: It will burn out our eyes for trying to see what's inside it. Burn them until there is nothing.

ADOLF: Nothing.

EVA: And we wouldn't like that too much.

> *Eva comes back to Adolf and stands in front of him. She puts her hands on the sides of his head.*

We like that, don't we?

ADOLF: Yes, we do.

EVA: It makes us happy.

ADOLF: Very happy.

EVA: And that's what we want to be all the time.

ADOLF: Yes.

EVA: We wouldn't like our hands to burn away.

ADOLF: No, we wouldn't.

EVA: Because hands can do such nice things.

ADOLF: Yes, they can.

EVA: We can touch our legs now, if we want to.

ADOLF: We can?

EVA: Go ahead.

> *Adolf tentatively touches one of Eva's legs.*

It's all right.

> *Adolf puts both his hands on her legs.*

ADOLF: Do we like that?

EVA: We like anything that makes us happy.

> *Eva leans over to kiss Adolf on the top of his head. Adolf runs his hands along her legs. Hold. Then blackout.*

Scene Four

It's night. The red light is subdued now, almost unnoticeable, but it will gradually build to the same intensity as in Scene Three by the end of this scene.

Nothing has changed. The floor is still littered with the smashed china and paper airplanes. Eva is still dressed in her slip. She stands, while Adolf sits on the sofa.

EVA: More than any other woman?

ADOLF: Of course I do.

EVA: More than all the women you've ever known?

ADOLF: Of course, Eva.

EVA: More than Geli?

ADOLF: Yes. But what has she got to do with —

EVA: Even more than Geli Raubal?

ADOLF: We agreed not to talk —

EVA: Agreements are made to be broken. Well, what about it?

ADOLF: What about what?

EVA: Don't play stupid with me.

ADOLF: I loved her in a different way.

EVA: I'll say you did.

ADOLF: She was my niece!

EVA: Was Unity Mitford your niece?

ADOLF: Of course not.

EVA: Was Hoffman's daughter your niece too?

ADOLF: Of course she wasn't.

EVA: You didn't think I knew about Hoffman arranging an affair between you and his daughter.

ADOLF: We were friends.

EVA: Then there's all the other women he arranged for you to meet.

ADOLF: It doesn't mean anything.

EVA: How come Geli Raubal killed herself when she found out you were taking me out?

ADOLF: We are not going to talk about this anymore. Do you understand?

EVA: How come she shot herself?

ADOLF: I forbid you to talk about her anymore.

EVA: You forbid me! You forbid me! I'm not one of your generals. I'm not Himmler or Goering. I'm Eva Braun, first lady of the Reich.

ADOLF: *(crossing his arms)* I refuse to talk about it.

EVA: How come you mourned for months after her death?

Adolf shakes his head.

How come you became a recluse for months, refusing to see anyone, including me, if she was just your niece?

Adolf smiles at her and shakes his head.

How come you had adjoining bedrooms in the Munich apartment?

Adolf shrugs his shoulders.

How come Geli never went out with any younger men? With men her own age? I can't believe that someone as beautiful as her couldn't find a man. It must have been terrible for the beautiful blonde to discover that all the men in the world had vanished, except for her uncle.

ADOLF: She was free to do what she wanted, with whoever she wanted.

EVA: How old was she when she first came to Munich?

ADOLF: Seventeen.

EVA: How much older were you?

ADOLF: Not that much.

EVA: Ten years? Twenty years?

ADOLF: I was her uncle and she was my niece and I was looking after her.

EVA: You looked after her so well, she blew her brains out.

ADOLF: I'm afraid you're wrong. She shot herself in the chest. Right here, just above the heart.

Adolf stands.

EVA: What's the difference. She still shot herself.

Adolf walks to where Eva stands.

ADOLF: Eva. Look into my eyes.

EVA: No, I don't want to.

Eva turns away but Adolf grabs her and makes her face him.

ADOLF: Look into them, Eva.

EVA: I don't have to if I don't want to.

ADOLF: I said look into them.

EVA: No, I don't want to. I don't.

ADOLF: Come on and have a look.

Eva looks and is caught in Adolf's hypnotic stare. She tries to break it but he holds her head in his hand until she is hypnotized.

Come on and look into my eyes, Eva. See what you can see in there. Don't be afraid. Don't ever be afraid to look inside. Now that's much better. Much better. Now, Eva, I want you to tell me what you see.

EVA: I see the whole world spinning through space.

ADOLF: And what's happening?

EVA: They're all waiting.

ADOLF: Who is?

EVA: The people. The people of the world. They're all waiting for him to come. They've been waiting for him to come for two thousand years.

ADOLF: And what are they doing?

EVA: They're on their knees. They're praying for him to come and save them from all the misery and suffering.

ADOLF: Do they know what the Messiah expects of them?

EVA: Yes, they know. To save them from the suffering there must be more suffering. To save those of pure blood we must eliminate those of impure blood.

ADOLF: And the people are prepared to follow his orders?

EVA: They are prepared to die if necessary.

ADOLF: They will sacrifice everything for the Reich?

EVA: Their bodies, their minds, whatever is necessary.

ADOLF: And they know the penalty if they fail? If they're not ready for the Messiah?

EVA: My Fuhrer, they know the penalty. They know he will leave them if they're not equal to his vision. They know the Messiah can only lead a race which is ready to be led.

ADOLF: And if they should fail the test he's set out for them?

EVA: The Messiah will destroy himself and the world.

ADOLF: Will he come again?

EVA: When the people are ready to be tested.

ADOLF: And when will that be?

EVA: I don't know, my Fuhrer. No one does.

ADOLF: Will the people ever be ready?

EVA: They hope they will be.

ADOLF: And if they aren't?

EVA: The whole world will burn. The people and everything they know will be destroyed in the flames and out of the ashes will grow a new race, a new people, equal to the vision of the Messiah.

Adolf breaks away from Eva and walks around her with his hands folded in front of him.

ADOLF: Tell us about the Messiah and women.

EVA: What is there to tell, my Fuhrer?

ADOLF: Tell us what they must understand.

EVA: They must understand he can never marry because the world is his wife. No woman could be his wife. Women disgust him.

ADOLF: Tell us something more.

EVA: Some women throw themselves in front of his Mercedes-Benz, hoping they will cause an accident. Hoping he will get out of the car and hold them.

ADOLF: Tell us about the young women.

EVA: Some rip open their blouses as he goes past in the street. Some come up to him dressed only in their raincoats, and then they open them, hoping —

ADOLF: Hoping for what?

EVA: That he will look at their bodies.

ADOLF: And if he does?

EVA: They are sent into ecstasy.

ADOLF: Into what?

EVA: Ecstasy, my Fuhrer.

ADOLF: Louder. I can't hear you.

EVA: *(louder)* Ecstasy, my Fuhrer.

ADOLF: I still can't hear you.

EVA: *(yelling)* ECSTASY!

ADOLF: Let's hear you this time!

EVA: *(screaming)* ECSTASY! ECSTASY! ECSTASY! ECSTASY!

ADOLF: All right. That's enough. Now, is there anything else the Messiah should know?

EVA: Some women make love with his photograph in the bed beside them.

> *Pause.*

Some call out his name in the labours of childbirth. And when the child is born they show the child his photograph.

> *Pause.*

Some call out his name when they come to their orgasm.

ADOLF: To their what?

EVA: Orgasm. Their climax.

ADOLF: I didn't hear that.

EVA: *(louder)* Orgasm.

ADOLF: I still didn't hear it.

EVA: *(even louder)* Orgasm!

ADOLF: We want to hear it this time!

EVA: *(screaming)* ORGASM!

ADOLF: WHAT DID YOU SAY?

EVA: I SAID ORGASM!

ADOLF: WHAT DID YOU SAY?

EVA: ORGASM!

ADOLF: SAY IT AGAIN!

EVA: ORGASM!

ADOLF: SAY IT AGAIN!

EVA: ORGASM!

ADOLF: AND AGAIN!

EVA: ORGASM! ORGASM! ORGASM! ORGASM! ORGASM! ORGASM!
ORGASM!

> *Eva walks around, her arm raised in salute. Adolf watches her in*
> *approval.*

ORGASM! ORGASM! ORGASM! ORGASM! ORGASM! ORGASM!
ORGASM! ORGASM! ORGASM! ORGASM! ORGASM! ORGASM!
ORGASM! ORGASM!

> *Adolf pushes down her arm and she stops screaming. He walks*
> *away from her and then stops downstage.*

ADOLF: And who is the Messiah living with now?

EVA: Eva Braun.

ADOLF: And is she beautiful?

EVA: Yes, very beautiful.

ADOLF: Is she clever?

EVA: Very clever.

ADOLF: Does he love her?

EVA: Yes, he does.

ADOLF: Does she love him?

EVA: She loves him very much.

ADOLF: Does she understand the Messiah?

EVA: Yes.

ADOLF: You fool! You've forgotten already. No woman could ever understand
him.

EVA: I'm sorry, my Fuhrer.

ADOLF: Why do you think he keeps her around?

EVA: Because he likes having her around.

ADOLF: Idiot!

EVA: I'm sorry, my Fuhrer. Is it because she's beautiful?

ADOLF: You're wrong again.

EVA: Is it because she's clever?

ADOLF: The answer is simple. She spreads her legs for him. Now get down on the floor.

>*Eva lies on her back.*

Spread your legs.

>*Eva spreads her legs.*

Farther.

>*Eva spreads her legs farther. Adolf stands between her legs.*

Farther still.

>*Eva spreads her legs as far as she can.*

You can do better than that.

EVA: No, I can't.

ADOLF: You know you can do better than that.

>*Eva tries to spread her legs farther but she can't.*

Come on. Really spread them this time.

EVA: I can't. I really can't.

ADOLF: Yes, you can.

EVA: I can't move any farther.

ADOLF: You can do better than that.

EVA: Not one more inch.

>*Adolf gets down on his knees between Eva's spread legs and tries to push them out farther.*

ADOLF: You know this isn't good enough.

EVA: I'm sorry, my Fuhrer.

ADOLF: You know there's other women who are better.

EVA: Yes, I know.

ADOLF: Much better.

EVA: You're hurting me.

ADOLF: Who are much more beautiful.

EVA: I can't go any farther.

ADOLF: Much more clever.

EVA: Please stop it. Please.

ADOLF: Much younger, more eager to please.

EVA: I'll do anything. Anything you want.

ADOLF: More eager to spread their legs.

>*Adolf stops pushing her legs apart. They're both exhausted.*

EVA: I'm sorry, my Fuhrer.

ADOLF: So am I. You know what you are?

Eva shakes her head.

You're a cunt. That's what you are.

Pause.

One cunt out of millions.

EVA: Forgive me, my Fuhrer.

ADOLF: It doesn't matter what happens to Eva Braun, does it?

EVA: I guess it doesn't.

ADOLF: She's not any different from any other woman. Repeat that.

EVA: She's not any different from any other woman.

ADOLF: She's nothing.

EVA: She's nothing.

ADOLF: A speck of dust on my arm is much more important. Repeat it.

EVA: A speck of dust on your arm is much more important. But why are you making me say these —

ADOLF: I didn't tell you to ask any questions. A bullet, a bomb, a soldier doing his duty, are all more important than her. Repeat that.

EVA: A bullet, a soldier doing —

ADOLF: A bomb!

EVA: A bullet, a bomb, a soldier doing his duty, are all more important than her.

ADOLF: She is only a woman. Only one body. One small pile of ashes. She isn't history. Eva Braun doesn't have the right to history. She hasn't earned her right yet. Repeat that.

Adolf gets up, goes to the cabinet and opens the top drawer.

EVA: She is only a woman. Only one body. One small pile of ashes. She isn't history. Eva Braun doesn't have the right to history. She hasn't earned her right yet.

Adolf takes a gun out of the drawer and walks back towards Eva, hiding the gun behind his back.

ADOLF: I have a present for you.

EVA: A present for me! How exciting!

ADOLF: You have to guess what it is.

EVA: Is it a pair of silk stockings?

Adolf shakes his head.

I know. It must be a dress from Vienna.

Adolf shakes his head again.

Then it must be shoes from Italy.

Adolf shakes his head again.

Then it's perfume. Is that what it is? Perfume from Paris?

ADOLF: It's something you're quite familiar with.

EVA: Something I'm familiar with but it's not clothes or shoes or perfume. I know what it is now. It's a camera.

ADOLF: No, it isn't.

EVA: All right, then tell me what it is.

ADOLF: You give up too easily.

EVA: It isn't any fun guessing when you don't give any clues.

ADOLF: I thought you'd know what it was.

Adolf brings the gun out from behind his back.

It's just like the one you tried to kill yourself with. Remember that?

EVA: Yes, I remember.

Adolf presses the barrel against Eva's neck, then he traces it down along her body, between her breasts and across her stomach.

What are you doing?

ADOLF: We're checking your body. We're checking it to see if it smells like history.

Adolf stops the gun at Eva's groin.

It's like being radioactive when you smell like that. And then this gun would start clicking like a geiger counter.

Adolf lifts the gun away.

Stand up.

Eva stands. Adolf hands her the gun.

Remember. You did it because he didn't pay enough attention to you.

EVA: Life wasn't worth living without him.

ADOLF: You must remember that he had his work to do.

EVA: He was constantly being seen with beautiful movie stars.

ADOLF: It was all for his country.

EVA: He could have telephoned. Or sent a postcard.

ADOLF: He had to win the people's confidence. He had to make them understand who he was.

EVA: I felt so alone in the world.

ADOLF: So did he.

EVA: Just like I do now.

ADOLF: Like he does all the time.

EVA: But I have the gun.

ADOLF: It must feel good in your hand.

EVA: It feels very good.

ADOLF: Raise the gun.

EVA: *(as she raises the gun)* As I slowly bring up the gun I'm thinking about that moment when he finds out I did it, that I shot myself, then he'll know how much I loved him. How much I really loved him.

ADOLF: Stop when you get to your heart.

EVA: That's right. I'll bring it up to my heart and stop because I know that's where he'd like me to shoot myself.

> *Eva points the gun at her chest, holding the gun with both hands.*

ADOLF: And now you move it closer.

EVA: This time I'll put it right against my chest.

ADOLF: Because you don't want to miss this time.

EVA: No, I don't.

ADOLF: This time you'll do it right, like Geli did.

EVA: That's how I want to do it.

ADOLF: Because you saw how much he cared for her.

EVA: Yes, I saw.

ADOLF: Because you saw how long he mourned for her.

EVA: Yes, I saw that too.

ADOLF: And so you decided to try it yourself.

EVA: That's right.

ADOLF: Are you ready now?

EVA: I'm ready.

ADOLF: All you have to do is squeeze the trigger.

EVA: I know.

ADOLF: Make sure you squeeze it nice and slow.

EVA: I will this time.

ADOLF: Goodbye.

EVA: I loved you. I really did.

ADOLF: Make sure you hit yourself this time.

> *Adolf sits down on the sofa to watch.*

EVA: I will. I'll do it right. I won't shoot myself through the neck this time. I don't want to spray blood all over the room and my clothes and scare you like I scared my mother and father and sisters. You won't find me sprawled on the bedroom rug, half-dead, like they did the last time.

ADOLF: That's my girl.

EVA: I just want it to happen fast. Last time everything seemed to move in slow-motion. I kept looking at the hole in the barrel like I'm doing right now and I kept thinking, Eva, this is it, this is really going to be the end, once you pull the trigger everything will be gone, and then I started to squeeze the trigger and that's when I seemed to step outside of myself. I was in the same room with Eva Braun, who was holding a gun, and I was watching her, and I knew I couldn't do anything to stop her and then she squeezed the trigger and the gun went off and the bullet came out of the barrel and it hit her in the neck and she put her right hand up to where she was hit and then she fell over.

Hold. Eva with the gun pointed at her chest. Adolf on the sofa, watching her, his hands folded in his lap. Then blackout.

Scene Five

They have been watching a movie. The light from the projector is still centred on the screen and it illuminates the room.

They are sitting on the sofa. Eva and Gretl are dressed in chic evening dresses. Martin and Gretl sit at either end of the sofa with Eva in the middle. They are all smoking cigarettes.

MARTIN: I certainly enjoyed that.

GRETL: I like anything Errol Flynn does.

MARTIN: *(to Eva)* Did you enjoy it?

EVA: It was all right

GRETL: *(to Eva)* Don't you just adore Errol Flynn?

EVA: He's all right.

GRETL: He's my idea of the perfect man. He's handsome, charming, intelligent. He's everything a woman could ever want.

EVA: I like John Barrymore better.

GRETL: You don't mean that, do you?

EVA: Of course I mean it.

GRETL: But did you see the way Errol Flynn fought all those men? He only had a sword and he killed them all.

EVA: John Barrymore could fight better with one hand tied behind his back.

GRETL: He could not.

EVA: Of course he could.

MARTIN: Now ladies, I'm afraid you're both wrong. Neither of them would make good soldiers, even though they're good actors. Now, let's have some more champagne.

Martin stands, holding a bottle of champagne.

EVA: Do you think we should?

MARTIN: *(filling her glass)* Of course we should. Champagne is made to be drunk, not left inside bottles.

EVA: But you know what the Chief thinks about drinking.

Martin fills Gretl's glass.

MARTIN: The Fuhrer understands that we all have to indulge once in a while.

GRETL: Stop worrying, Eva. You know he doesn't mind what you do.

EVA: But if he should come in here and find us like this.

MARTIN: He'll be quite a long time with that meeting. When I left they were still discussing the first report. To put it more precisely, the Fuhrer was telling them what should have been done in the first place. But now, I want to propose a toast.

They all raise their glasses.

EVA: To what?

MARTIN: To the beautiful women in this room.

GRETL: Thank you.

EVA: Salud.

They all drink. Martin stands in front of the movie screen, so he is directly in the light from the projector.

MARTIN: Now that's much better. Yes, it's definitely much better. Which reminds me of a story. It seems there was this man who was sent to Dachau for some kind of offence, I can't remember exactly what it was. No doubt it was something particularly nasty. Anyway, they had been relieved of their valuables and clothes and they were standing in line, waiting for their heads to be shaved. Now this disturbed the man and so he stepped out of line and walked up to the officer in charge of the operation. I suppose he was used to more individual, more personal treatment on the outside. Perhaps he expected his own barber. You know how these Jews expect the world to provide them with everything, even when they have committed crimes against the state. But do you know what the man asked? He asked the officer if he could keep his hair.

GRETL: *(genuinely astounded)* He didn't.

MARTIN: Yes, he did.

GRETL: I hope the officer struck him for his insubordination.

MARTIN: Normally he would have been beaten on the spot by the guards for even stepping out of line. But the man's naiveté astounded the officer for a moment and he didn't know what to do. Understandably, I would say. He finally asked the man why he shouldn't have his head shaved, because it happened to be one of the camp regulations. But do you know what the man said then?

GRETL: No. What did he say?

MARTIN: First, I think we need some more champagne.

> *Martin refills Gretl's glass and Eva's glass and then his own.*

GRETL: The champagne can wait. Tell us what the man said.

MARTIN: In good time, my dear. Good things, like champagne, aren't made quickly.

GRETL: But you do this all the time with your stories.

MARTIN: And that's why you enjoy them so much.

> *He resumes his stance in front of the screen.*

Now. Here we have one man asking to be made an exception to the regulations, an exception to all the men standing in the line, an exception to all the men who had already entered the camp. His audacity was tremendous.

EVA: But what did he say?

MARTIN: He said he couldn't possibly have his head shaved because his skin was sensitive and ever since he was a boy, his mother had kept him out of the sun in the summer for fear of creating a skin rash. You see, he was afraid that with too much sun, a rash would break out on his head.

> *Martin laughs tremendously at this. Eva and Gretl smile.*

EVA: Is that it?

GRETL: There must be more.

MARTIN: There certainly is. This officer was a man with a sense of humour and so he replied that the officials had thought of just this problem when they were planning the camp and they had picked Dachau for its geographical position.

GRETL: For its position?

MARTIN: Yes, because as he told the man, Dachau has a very mild climate, in fact, the mildest in the Reich and in the summertime, they have quite a lot of rain.

GRETL: Did he believe that?

MARTIN: Not only did he believe it but he asked the officer if they would be supplied with caps to protect their heads from the rain.

> *Gretl laughs.*

GRETL: He didn't!

MARTIN: Oh, yes he did. The officer managed to keep a straight face until the man rejoined the line and then he couldn't control himself from laughing any longer.

> *Gretl is laughing uncontrollably now. Eva smiles as she lights a cigarette.*

And when the officer had control of himself he told some guards what the man had asked him and they burst into laughter and that started the officer laughing again. You can imagine it didn't take long for the story to spread through the camp. For weeks after that, one guard only had to scratch his head at another guard and they both would burst out laughing. The prisoner was constantly asked by the other prisoners if the sun was too hot for him.

> *The telephone rings and Martin steps out of the light of the projector and answers it.*

Yes. *(pause)* Yes. *(pause)* Very well. Thank you.

> *He puts the receiver down.*

The meeting's over. The Fuhrer is coming.

> *Eva immediately stubs out her cigarette, stands and picks up her ashtray, and empties it in the wastebasket. Gretl has another drag on her cigarette before she puts it out.*

> *Martin stands in front of the screen, talking with them as he casually sips his champagne.*

EVA: Come on. Don't just stand there. We have to clean this place up.

MARTIN: We can't get rid of the smoke, at least not before he gets here. So we might as well relax. He knows we all smoke and drink.

EVA: But there's no point in making things worse.

MARTIN: No point in trying to hide what's obvious either.

EVA: What about the glasses?

MARTIN: Leave them. If there's any problem, it'll be my fault.

EVA: All right. But don't say I didn't warn you.

GRETL: You worry too much. Remember when we were having a smoke downstairs and he came down unexpectedly, so you had to sit on it? That was so funny.

EVA: That wasn't so funny. It burnt a hole through my dress.

GRETL: I thought I'd burst out laughing from the look on your face.

EVA: I don't know what you're talking about. I had perfect control of my face, like any good actress.

> *Adolf opens the door and comes into the room. He stands in front of the screen beside Martin.*

ADOLF: What's this all about?

EVA: *(innocent)* What's what all about?

ADOLF: All these glasses and bottles.

MARTIN: I'm afraid the champagne was my idea.

ADOLF: I'm sure it was.

MARTIN: How did the meeting go?

ADOLF: Badly. I don't want to talk about it. *(to Eva)* How was the movie tonight?

EVA: It was all right.

GRETL: It was sensational. You should have seen the way Errol Flynn fought all these men and killed them by himself!

ADOLF: I'm glad you enjoyed yourselves with the movie. *(to Martin)* We leave for Berlin immediately.

MARTIN: Very well, my Fuhrer. I'll go and get a few things ready. If you'll excuse me, ladies, I'll say goodnight now.

GRETL: Goodnight, Herr Bormann.

> *Martin leaves.*

EVA: Do you have to go at this time of the night?

ADOLF: Something very important has come up.

EVA: Can't it wait until morning?

ADOLF: I said that something very important has come up. Didn't you hear me the first time?

EVA: Yes, I did.

> *Pause. Adolf paces up and down in front of the screen, his hands folded in front of him.*

GRETL: *(to Eva)* I think I really should be going.

EVA: Feeling tired?

GRETL: As a matter of fact, I am. So I'll say goodnight now.

EVA: Goodnight, Gretl.

ADOLF: You are not to leave the room.

GRETL: But I thought that you would rather . . .

ADOLF: You mean she told you to go.

EVA: I never did any such thing.

ADOLF: You nodded to her. You made a sign to her.

EVA: How can you say something like that when you know it isn't true?

ADOLF: It's true if I say it's true.

> *Pause. Adolf keeps pacing up and down. Eva stands now in the light from the projector and watches him walk. Gretl sits at the table, watching both of them.*

EVA: *(softer)* How long will you be gone?

ADOLF: As long as it is necessary.

EVA: Can I come?

ADOLF: No.

EVA: Why not?

ADOLF: Because I want you to stay here.

EVA: Maybe I want to go with you.

> *Pause. Adolf shrugs his shoulders as he paces.*

EVA: Gretl should be able to go to sleep if she wants.

ADOLF: She can't.

EVA: You have no right.

ADOLF: I have every right in the world.

EVA: How do you expect us to . . .

Adolf stops pacing and looks at her.

ADOLF: Expect us what?

EVA: Nothing.

ADOLF: Expect us to do what?

EVA: It doesn't matter now.

The phone rings and Adolf picks it up.

ADOLF: Yes. *(pause)* I'll be right down.

He puts the receiver down.

I have to go now.

He doesn't move out of the darkness.

EVA: I'll come with you downstairs and say goodbye.

ADOLF: You can say that here.

EVA: Will you phone me?

ADOLF: Yes, I'll phone you.

EVA: At least once a day? You promise?

ADOLF: Yes.

Eva leaves the light of the projector and goes to Adolf. She hugs him but he doesn't respond. She steps back, looks at him and then kisses him on the forehead.

ADOLF: Goodnight.

Adolf walks through the light of the projector and leaves. Eva steps into the light. Gretl gets up from the table and stands beside her.

EVA: I really should go and see him off.

GRETL: No, you won't. You'll sit down and be a good girl.

EVA: Everytime he goes somewhere, I always feel as if he's never coming back. What if something happened? I didn't even say goodbye to him.

GRETL: You said goodbye to him.

EVA: Not really.

GRETL: Stop worrying. Nothing's going to happen to him.

EVA: Do you think so?

GRETL: Of course I do. Now sit down and have some more champagne.

EVA: All right.

GRETL: Just because everyone else leaves, doesn't mean the party has to stop for us.

> *Eva sits on the sofa. Gretl fills Eva's glass and then refills her own.*

Let's have some more of this delicious champagne. There's no reason in the world why we can't have a good time.

EVA: I guess so.

GRETL: Eva, darling, we could have the maids bring up some caviar from the cellar. Or we could have them make us some of those delicious little sandwiches. Do you want me to ring them?

EVA: No, I don't feel like it right now.

GRETL: All right.

> *Pause. Gretl wanders around the room with her glass in her hand.*

GRETL: Herr Bormann's story was quite amusing, wasn't it?

EVA: It bored me.

GRETL: It did?

EVA: That was the second time I've heard it.

GRETL: I think I could hear it a second time. It's the way he tells his stories that I enjoy.

EVA: He's as boring as his stories are.

GRETL: I thought they amused the Fuhrer.

EVA: They do, but that doesn't mean they amuse me too.

> *Gretl picks up the gun which is on top of the cabinet.*

GRETL: I didn't know you kept a gun.

EVA: The Chief makes me keep it for self-protection.

GRETL: Is it loaded?

> *Gretl points the gun at someone in the audience.*

EVA: Very definitely.

GRETL: It feels good in my hand. They say to shoot well all you have to do is keep a steady hand.

EVA: I suppose they do say that.

GRETL: I wonder what it's like to kill someone, to kill a complete stranger.

EVA: I guess you wouldn't know until you did it.

> *Gretl advances downstage, still pointing the gun at someone in the audience.*

GRETL: Say that stranger was someone who didn't matter, who no one would miss if he lived or not. Say a Jew or something like that. And if you were on a roof and you had him lined up in your sights and all you had to do was squeeze the trigger. And say you had all the time in the world to do it, that nothing could interfere with you killing him. It would be interesting to experience what you would feel then, because you decide when you kill him. All you do is squeeze the trigger. And you decide how you'll kill him. Should it be right between the eyes? Or maybe in the stomach would be better. They say when you're hit in the stomach that it's much more painful, much slower. Or you could shoot him in the back, right between the shoulder blades, trying to get him through the heart. That would be a difficult shot, wouldn't it? Especially if you were shooting from any kind of angle.

EVA: Maybe you better put it down.

GRETL: I guess when you can kill someone, when there's no chance of anything going wrong, then you're God for a moment. Nietzsche probably said something like that.

EVA: I don't know if he did, but I wish you wouldn't wave it around like that. They're dangerous to fool around with.

GRETL: Afraid of me making a mistake?

Gretl turns and comes back to Eva.

EVA: What do you mean?

GRETL: Afraid of me shooting myself accidentally?

EVA: Why would you do that?

GRETL: Mistakes can happen.

Gretl sits beside Eva on the sofa.

EVA: They will if you keep waving that gun around.

GRETL: Some people shoot themselves when they don't mean to. Others shoot themselves when they want to and make a mess of it.

EVA: Yes, some people do.

GRETL: Do you think suicide is another form of murder?

EVA: I don't know.

GRETL: I wonder if it is.

EVA: I'm not a philosopher.

GRETL: Neither am I. And here I am talking away and my champagne is probably going flat.

Pause. Gretl gets up, goes to the cabinet and picks up her glass. Then she sits on the sofa.

If Mother could only see us now.

EVA: I was thinking that she and Father should come out to the Berghof for a visit sometime.

GRETL: That would be nice.

EVA: It would, wouldn't it?

GRETL: They'd never believe it. It's so beautiful up here in the mountains.

EVA: And on a clear day you can see the church towers of Salzburg.

GRETL: I know. Remember the day you first met the Fuhrer and you asked Father at dinner what he thought about him?

EVA: Didn't he say something very serious, like he's just another young upstart who wants to run the world and doesn't have any idea of how to do it?

GRETL: And if he'd known that you had met that day, I think he would have said quite a lot more.

EVA: He certainly would have.

GRETL: It was amazing that you went out with him for so long and they never suspected a thing.

EVA: It was so exciting then, wasn't it?

GRETL: Yes, those were the days all right.

> *Pause. They both sip at their champagne.*

EVA: Oh, by the way, how are you and Herr Fegelin coming along?

GRETL: Quite well, thank you.

EVA: The Chief thinks he would be a good match for you.

GRETL: He never stops match-making, does he? If it's not his dogs, it's people.

EVA: An SS general, my dear, is nothing to sneeze at. Especially someone as handsome as him.

GRETL: And don't forget his charm. That man is so charming I think he could make a mountain move if he wanted it to.

EVA: So when can we expect an announcement?

GRETL: I thought we could make one together.

EVA: What do you mean?

GRETL: I thought maybe we could have a double ceremony.

EVA: Don't be silly, Gretl.

GRETL: I'm not being silly.

EVA: But what an idea. The Chief is far too busy right now to think of anything like that. He has so much on his mind these days that —

GRETL: He worries enough about other people getting married.

EVA: He likes playing the matchmaker. It's a second nature to him.

GRETL: What about you? What are you going to do?

EVA: Don't worry. After all this is over, the Chief and I will be married. But not one minute before that. He has already bought the property in Linz and that's where we'll retire.

GRETL: Are you sure?

EVA: Of course I'm sure.

GRETL: Are you positive?

EVA: Of course.

GRETL: Absolutely?

EVA: Why are you asking all these questions?

GRETL: Because, dear sister, I think we're going to lose.

EVA: Don't be ridiculous! The idea that the Chief would lose the war is absurd! He won't allow them to lose it this time, no matter what! Even if all his generals committed blunders, he'd still win. You see, he's taken that into account with his plans, so there's no way that . . .

GRETL: I know something we can do.

EVA: What?

GRETL: Let's look through your photo album.

EVA: All right. That's a really good idea.

> *Eva goes to the cabinet, opens a drawer and takes out her photo album. Gretl lounges on the sofa and twirls the gun on her forefinger. Eva sits beside her on the sofa.*

EVA: *(opening the album)* We haven't done this in a long time, have we? The last time we stayed up all night and watched the sun come up in the morning.

GRETL: Yes, that's what we did.

EVA: Let's do it again. We'll stay up all night and drink lots and lots of champagne and watch the sun come up over the mountains. It's so beautiful when it comes up because then I feel I can go to sleep. I hate going to sleep when it's still dark outside.

GRETL: A lot of people find it hard to sleep these days.

EVA: I've taken so many photos since you last saw the album, I don't know where to begin.

GRETL: In fact, they say there's a lot more nightmares.

> *Gretl continues to spin the gun around her forefinger. She doesn't pay any attention to Eva and the photograph album.*

EVA: Here's some I took this summer when we were on a picnic up by the Teahouse. You see, there's Goebbels and his wife and here's some pictures of their children. Aren't they adorable? And there's Bormann and his wife. And look at this one. The Chief looks so relaxed. Here's one of Blondi, his dog. And look at this one of the Chief. I wanted him to take off his hat but he wouldn't because the sun was so bright that day. And here's another one of him. He looks so sweet, doesn't he? You know, he can be really sweet when he wants to be. This one I made him sit up and look serious because he didn't feel like being serious at all that afternoon and so I wanted to see if he could do it. He did it quite well, don't you think? I told him as I was taking the shot that he had to hold it, that a really good actor always has control of his expressions, but after the click of the shutter, after I took the shot, he burst out laughing.

> *The light from the projector is cut. Blackout.*

alias

CHARACTERS

LONE RANGER, thirty

TONTO, thirty

AMY, twenty

REBECCA, twenty-eight

ALIAS

Bright white desert light. There is a pile of stones in the centre, a dead tree at one side and a few huge boulders at the back.

RANGER: *(off)* I better check it out first.

TONTO: *(off)* Good idea, Kimosabee.

RANGER: *(off)* You stay here until I give the all clear.

TONTO: *(off)* I keep you covered.

> *The Lone Ranger crawls on stage with both guns drawn. He stops, looks around. A twig snaps. He scrambles behind a boulder.*

RANGER: You hear that?

TONTO: *(off)* Yeah.

RANGER: What do you think it was?

TONTO: *(off)* Don't know.

> *The Ranger peeks over the boulder, then ducks behind it.*

RANGER: There's nothing out there.

> *Pause. As he looks over the boulder again, another twig snaps. He ducks.*

There it is again.

TONTO: *(off)* Maybe it animal.

RANGER: It could be a trap. It could be Willy Horton and his gang of rustlers. Or Dirty Sam and his band of desperadoes. Or Diamond Daisy, alias Queen of Spades, who would rather shoot a man than say hello.

TONTO: *(off)* You scared?

RANGER: Of course not!

TONTO: *(off)* Cause you sound like it.

RANGER: We've put a lot of outlaws behind bars, Tonto. Any one of them could be out there. With his finger on the trigger.

> *Pause.*

TONTO: *(off)* Kimosabee.

RANGER: All right. What is it?

TONTO: *(off)* I got something to tell you.

RANGER: Not now. I have to think.

TONTO: *(off)* It important.

> *Pause. The Ranger looks over the boulder, then ducks behind it.*

(off) It real important.

RANGER: All right. What is it?

TONTO: *(off)* You know twig that snapped once, then twice?

RANGER: Yeah.

TONTO: *(off)* I stand on twig.

RANGER: You what?

TONTO: *(off)* I been standing on twig all the time.

RANGER: You're joking.

TONTO: *(off)* I wish I was.

> *The Ranger walks out from behind the boulder. Tonto comes on, carrying two pairs of saddlebags and dragging a saddle behind him.*

RANGER: How could you do something so stupid?

TONTO: It accident.

> *Tonto puts down the saddle and saddlebags.*

RANGER: You could have been killed.

TONTO: Yeah.

RANGER: It's lucky I have good nerves. Any other man would have shot first and asked questions later.

> *Pause. He twirls both guns on his fingers and then drops them into the holsters.*

TONTO: Except.

RANGER: Except what?

TONTO: I go fix us some grub.

> *Tonto turns to go but the Ranger puts his hand on Tonto's shoulder.*

RANGER: Now just a minute. What were you going to say?

TONTO: Nothing.

RANGER: Don't start sulking.

TONTO: I don't sulk.

RANGER: Tell me what it was.

TONTO: You won't like it.

RANGER: I thought we said we'd always be honest with each other.

TONTO: It make you look stupid.

RANGER: That isn't important

TONTO: You said you didn't kill me because of your good nerves.

RANGER: That's right.

TONTO: But you forget one thing.

RANGER: What's that?

TONTO: You have no bullets left in gun. Someone steal all your silver bullets, just like someone steal our horses.

RANGER: I only nodded off for a minute.

TONTO: You still asleep when sun wakes me.

RANGER: It can happen to anyone. We'd been riding for days after those outlaws.

TONTO: I never sleep when on guard.

RANGER: I know you don't.

TONTO: Your fault we have to walk.

RANGER: I know.

TONTO: Your fault we not catch outlaws.

RANGER: We'll catch them, don't you worry about that.

TONTO: If they lie down and wait, then maybe we catch them.

> *Pause. The Lone Ranger walks to a boulder and stands by it with his arms crossed.*

Kimosabee sulking now.

RANGER: I am not.

TONTO: Yes, you are.

RANGER: Leave me alone.

TONTO: You sure look funny if outlaws were waiting for you. Lone Ranger, heap big fighter for law and order, heap big protector of women and children from no good swearing, drinking, spitting, fucking outlaws and he don't even have one silver bullet in his gun. Ha ha ha ha ha ha ha ha ha ha ha!

RANGER: Stop it.

TONTO: You sure look stupid!

RANGER: Cut it out.

TONTO: Ha ha ha ha ha ha ha ha ha ha ha ha!

RANGER: I'm warning you.

TONTO: That's a good one.

> *Pause. The Ranger undoes the snaps to his shirt and takes it off. Then he undoes the buckle to his gunbelt and drops it to the ground.*

What are you doing?

> *The Ranger raises his leg and tries to pull off his boot. Tonto walks over to him.*

What are you taking your clothes off for?

> *The Ranger raises his other leg and tries to pull off the boot but he can't.*

TONTO: Let me help you.

> *Tonto pulls off the boot.*

RANGER: Thanks.

> *The Ranger raises his other leg and Tonto pulls off the boot.*

TONTO: Why are you taking off your clothes?

> *The Ranger takes off his white pants. Underneath he wears a pair of long underwear.*

RANGER: I don't know. I feel like it.

TONTO: Are they dirty?

RANGER: A little bit.

TONTO: Cause they look filthy enough.

RANGER: You think so?

TONTO: It's been a week since you changed.

RANGER: You're right. They are filthy.

TONTO: Do you want some clean clothes?

RANGER: I didn't know we had any.

TONTO: Let me look

> *Tonto opens a saddlebag and pulls out a dirty shirt and pants. He opens the other saddlebag.*

RANGER: Sometimes I wish I could become a different person with a different past and future, just by changing my clothes. You ever feel like that?

TONTO: Here it is.

> *Tonto walks up to him, holding a clean shirt and pants.*

RANGER: You ever feel like that?

TONTO: Like what, Kimosabee?

RANGER: Nothing. I was thinking out loud.

TONTO: I get some grub ready.

> *Tonto comes downstage and kneels by the saddlebags.*

To hell with that right now.

> *Tonto looks around to see if the Lone Ranger heard him but he's busy pulling on his pants. Tonto sits against the saddle.*

Good. Him not like to hear swear words. But feet sure hurt like hell. *(he unlaces moccasin)* We must have walked twenty miles today. But after first mile, it all feel the same. *(he pulls off the moccasin and rubs his foot)*

Aaaaaaaaaaaahhhhhh! That feels good. They sure don't make moccasins like they used to. Them lousy for walking. Aaaaahhhhh! Foot sure stink though. Stink bad as buffalo pie. Better wash them in creek tonight. Now's let see. We got three days before we get to Wasteland. *(he inspects the moccasin)* Sure hope you last, moccasin. We have to get to Wasteland so we can make silver bullets. Don't have to dig for it cause big chunks of silver lay on ground. Don't have to do anything there except relax. Lots of fruit on trees. Plenty game in forest, plenty fish in stream. There is legend about Wasteland. Long ago, thunderbirds used to rule sky. Them very mighty, very beautiful. They used to shit silver around Wasteland and they make earth rich with it and rich enough to grow everything ten times better than anywhere else in world. But now all thunderbirds gone. Them fly away. Far away. No one know where they go.

REBECCA: *(off)* Help! Help!

RANGER: What's that?

TONTO: Sounds like someone calling for help.

REBECCA: *(off)* Help! Help!

> *The Ranger is dressed now except for his gunbelt, which he buckles up as he comes down to Tonto.*

RANGER: We better rescue her.

TONTO: You go, my feet are killing me.

RANGER: Come on, that's no excuse.

TONTO: I'm staying here.

REBECCA.   *(off)* Help! Someone help me!

RANGER: There's a woman out there. Alone. Helpless.

TONTO: So go and help her.

REBECCA: *(off)* Somebody help me! Please!

RANGER: Well, I'm going.

TONTO: Good luck.

> *The Ranger goes off with both guns drawn. Tonto unlaces his other moccasin.*

Half the time we go rescue someone, it not even worth it. But one thing about him, he always goes. I go most of the time but what the hell, I got my own life too.

> *As Tonto talks, a penis comes around the boulder, crawling on its hands and knees, and heads for him. Amy is inside the penis costume.*

Most people think you should come running whenever they want and that gets me mad, cause if they thought about things beforehand, then they wouldn't get into trouble. *(Tonto takes off his moccasin)* And another thing. Everytime someone wants to give us a reward he says no. What's wrong with few bucks? We all have to live somehow.

Amy nudges the penis' head against Tonto's back. She can see through two eye slits.

TONTO: Cut it out, Kimosabee.

Amy nudges Tonto again.

Stop joking around.

Amy nudges him again and Tonto grabs the penis around its head.

Got you!

Tonto realizes it isn't the Ranger and lets go.

What the hell!

Amy nuzzles the head of the penis against Tonto's chest but he backs away.

Get away from me.

Tonto stands and Amy moves after him.

Stay right where you are. Stay put. I'm warning you.

Tonto pulls his gun, then puts it back in his holster. He pulls his knife.

Don't come any closer or else . . .

Tonto keeps backing up but Amy keeps following him.

Goddamn it! What do you want?

A gunshot is heard offstage. Both Tonto and Amy freeze for a moment.

Did you hear that? My friend could be in trouble . . . I should . . .

AMY: *(barely audible)* . . .irsty . . .

TONTO: What did you say?

AMY: *(a little louder)* . . .irsty . . .

TONTO: Can you say it louder?

Amy nudges the penis' head against the canteen tied to the saddle.

TONTO: I get it. You're thirsty! *(he crosses to the saddle)* You won't bite me, will you?

Amy shakes its head no. Tonto undoes the canteen and holds it up to the mouth, so Amy can drink.

You sure are thirsty.

Tonto runs his hand along the back of the penis, as if it was a horse. The bright white desert light begins to redden as sunset approaches.

You don't want to drink too much at once. It's bad for you.

Tonto takes the canteen away from Amy.

So what do you have to say now?

AMY: Thirsty!

TONTO: But you have to wait.

>*Amy nuzzles the penis' head against Tonto's leg for more water.*

REBECCA: *(off)* Put your hands on my breasts.

RANGER: *(off)* I can't do that.

REBECCA: (off) Why not?

RANGER: *(off)* It isn't right.

>*Amy raises the head of the penis at the sound of Rebecca's voice.*
>*She begins to crawl off.*

TONTO: *(to Amy)* Where you going?

REBECCA: *(off)* Then I'll put my hand in your pants.

RANGER: *(off)* You can't do that!

TONTO: You can't leave like this. I want you to meet my friend.

>*Amy goes off and Tonto follows her off.*

REBECCA: *(off)* But you'll like it.

RANGER: *(off)* Stay away from me!

REBECCA: *(off)* All I have to do is unzip your pants and . . .

>*We hear what sounds like a punch or a slap and then muttering.*

>*Tonto comes on just as the Ranger enters from the other side,*
>*carrying an unconscious Rebecca.*

RANGER: What a maniac!

TONTO: What happened?

RANGER: I had to knock her out.

>*Tonto crosses to him.*

TONTO: You hit her?

RANGER: I had to do it, Tonto.

>*He helps the Ranger lower Rebecca to the ground, where they*
>*lay her against the saddle.*

TONTO: You hit a woman?

RANGER: She forced me. She tried to put her hand in my pants . . .

>*Rebecca wears a cowboy hat, pants, shirt, cowboy boots and has*
>*a gunbelt and a gun in its holster.*

TONTO: What was she screaming about?

RANGER: She scared a rattlesnake sunning himself on a rock.

TONTO: And gunshot?

RANGER: I used her gun to kill the rattler. Then she put her arms around me.
She was shaking.

TONTO: I can imagine.

> *Pause. Rebecca moans and rolls her head to one side. Tonto kneels in front of her with the canteen.*

TONTO: Maybe she needs some water.

RANGER: No! She doesn't.

TONTO: But it might bring her around.

RANGER: She's fine like that.

> *Pause. Tonto stands, takes a drink from the canteen. The sunset is over now and the red and orange light changes gradually to blue evening light.*

She said I needed a reward. Then she kissed me on the mouth.

TONTO: How about that.

RANGER: And as she kissed me, she kept saying, I want you to —

TONTO: To what?

RANGER: You know.

TONTO: Kiss her?

RANGER: No.

TONTO: She wanted you to put your arms around her.

RANGER: Not that.

TONTO: What then?

RANGER: You know what. I want you to —

TONTO: Caress me?

RANGER: No.

TONTO: Grab my breasts?

RANGER: It has four letters.

TONTO: Love me?

RANGER: No. Tonto.

TONTO: I give up.

RANGER: You know what it is.

TONTO: You'll have to tell me.

RANGER: Quit horsing around.

TONTO: I don't know what you're talking about.

> *Pause. Rebecca moans again.*

RANGER: She kept saying, I want you to . . .

TONTO: And it has four letters?

RANGER: Yeah.

TONTO: And it's dirty word?

RANGER: Yeah.

TONTO: And it has something to do with sex?

RANGER: Yes. Yes!

TONTO: I don't know what it could be.

RANGER: Animals do it all the time!

TONTO: What kind of animals?

RANGER: Horses. Cows. Dogs.

TONTO: They do a lot of things.

RANGER: It's how they make little animals.

TONTO: You mean fucking?

RANGER: That's it!

TONTO: Why didn't you say so in first place?

RANGER: I tried.

TONTO: She wanted you and her . . . right here in desert . . . how about that.

> *Pause. Rebecca moans again.*

Looks like she's coming around.

RANGER: Do you think she'll try something?

TONTO: No.

RANGER: I hope not. I think I'll go to sleep.

> *The Lone Ranger walks up to a boulder.*

TONTO: Do you know what happened to me while you were gone?

> *Tonto follows him.*

RANGER: Can't it wait until morning?

> *The Ranger sits, leans against the boulder.*

TONTO: You'll never believe it.

RANGER: You take the first watch.

TONTO: Sure, Kimosabee. But it would only take minute of your time.

> *Rebecca wakes up.*

REBECCA: Did I hear a voice? Or is this a dream?

TONTO: *(to Ranger)* How about it?

RANGER: Let me sleep.

> *Rebecca turns, sees them.*

REBECCA: Say!

> *She gets up, walks up to them.*

You're the cowboy who punched me!

RANGER: If you let me explain —

Rebecca kicks the Ranger in the leg.

REBECCA: No one treats me like that!

Tonto takes hold of her.

RANGER: That hurt.

REBECCA: So did your punch.

RANGER: I'm sorry I did it but —

REBECCA: Just because you're afraid of having fun, doesn't give you any right —

TONTO: Easy, lady.

REBECCA: I want you to let go of me.

Pause. Tonto lets go of her arms.

RANGER: I'm sorry it happened.

REBECCA: Some men have given me goldmines for a lot less. It's the last time I'll show my gratitude.

TONTO: I guess he should have let that rattler bite you, eh?

REBECCA: Stay out of this, injun.

RANGER: You shouldn't say things like that.

REBECCA: I'll say what I want, where I want it!

Pause. She walks to the saddle.

TONTO: Although I don't think snake would have killed you, what with all the poison you already have inside.

REBECCA: Very funny.

Tonto slowly walks to her.

TONTO: What are you doing out here?

REBECCA: What business is it of yours?

TONTO: The desert is big place.

REBECCA: Seems pretty crowded to me.

Pause. The Ranger pulls his hat tighter over his head and tries to sleep.

TONTO: Are you lost?

REBECCA: Do I look it?

TONTO: Where's your horse?

REBECCA: He ran away.

TONTO: The snake scare him?

REBECCA: Something else did.

She sits on the saddle and takes a small pipe from her pocket.

TONTO: Like what?

REBECCA: Why all these questions?

TONTO: Just curious.

> *Pause. Rebecca strikes a match and lights her pipe.*

REBECCA: So what do you cowboys do?

TONTO: We help people. Capture outlaws.

REBECCA: I see. *(pause)* Can't be much money in that.

TONTO: There isn't.

REBECCA: So what's your angle?

TONTO: Angle?

REBECCA: What do you get out of it?

TONTO: Out of what?

REBECCA: Helping people. All that business.

TONTO: I don't know. Never really thought about it.

REBECCA: Why does he wear that mask?

TONTO: The mask?

REBECCA: And those white clothes?

TONTO: I don't know.

REBECCA: Seems stupid to me.

TONTO: Why all these questions?

REBECCA: Just curious.

> *Tonto, who stands behind her, pulls out his knife, puts his arm around her and puts the knife against her throat.*

TONTO: Curiosity almost kill cat too.

REBECCA: What's the idea!

TONTO: You should watch what you call people.

REBECCA: Let go of me!

TONTO: They might get wrong idea about you. They might slice your throat or stick you in gut!

> *As Tonto takes his arm from her neck, he takes her gun. He puts the gun inside his belt, the knife back in its sheath.*

REBECCA: You took my gun.

TONTO: What do you expect? I'm no-good Indian.

REBECCA: I'd like it back.

TONTO: Maybe tomorrow.

REBECCA: I really would . . . so . . . what's your name?

TONTO: Tonto.

REBECCA: How long have you been riding with your friend?

TONTO: Long time now.

Rebecca stands, walks to Tonto.

REBECCA: You're not like him, are you?

TONTO: Him good man. I good man half the time.

REBECCA: Why don't you come back into town with me?

TONTO: Why should I?

Rebecca takes off her hat and undoes her hair. It falls down her back, long and beautiful. She shakes it.

REBECCA: I was thinking. I have a nice saloon called the Golden Triangle, where I could set you up as something special for the ladies. You could wear a leather loincloth, a bear-claw necklace and a head-dress of eagle feathers. The finest eagle feathers money could buy.

TONTO: And what would I do?

REBECCA: All you would do is strut around the casino, past the roulette wheel and blackjack tables, until you pick up a woman.

TONTO: Then what?

REBECCA: Then you take her upstairs. Wait a minute! Your bed could be built out of thousands of animal bones. Bear, deer, wolf, cougar, wolverine. Whatever you wanted. And on top of each bedpost you'd have a buffalo skull. Can't you see it? The ladies would love it!

TONTO: So I just screw them?

REBECCA: And take their money.

TONTO: How many?

REBECCA: As many as you want, cowboy. It's like a dream come true, isn't it? So have we got a deal?

She offers her hand to shake.

TONTO: I talk with Kimosabee first. See what he say.

REBECCA: You know what he'll say.

TONTO: Him wise man.

REBECCA: You have a mind of your own.

TONTO: Me sleep on it.

REBECCA: Think of the money you'll make. A fifty-fifty split.

TONTO: Me wait.

Tonto sits on the saddle.

REBECCA: You won't have to ride through freezing blizzards or across boiling deserts. You won't have to go hungry. You'll have everything you ever wanted. It's a chance of a lifetime. You'll never have another one like this.

Tonto shakes his head. Amy, in the penis costume, comes around the boulder, crawls past the sleeping Lone Ranger and heads for Tonto.

What's the percentage in letting some cowboy drag you over hell's half acre?

TONTO: Him try and keep law and order.

REBECCA: Everyone takes as much as they can and then clears out before they're caught . . .

Amy nudges Tonto's back with the head of the penis.

TONTO: Where have you been? Why did you leave like that?

REBECCA: You must think you're smart, running off on me like that.

Amy backs away from Rebecca.

TONTO: Do you know this animal?

REBECCA: *(following)* What's the big idea? Do you realize how much money you've cost me?

TONTO: Where did you meet?

REBECCA: Come on. Answer me!

Rebecca kicks the penis in the side. Amy moans.

TONTO: Stop that.

Tonto walks up on the other side of the penis.

REBECCA: *(slapping it)* You no good double-crossing varmint!

TONTO: You don't need to hit it!

REBECCA: *(slapping it)* Stay out of this!

Tonto grabs Rebecca's arms.

TONTO: I said you don't need —

REBECCA: I'll do whatever I want with it!

TONTO: You don't own it.

REBECCA: Yes, I do.

AMY: No, you don't!

TONTO: It said something.

REBECCA: It can do a lot of things.

Tonto lets go of Rebecca.

TONTO: Can you say it again?

AMY: No, you don't!

TONTO: Can you understand me?

He kneels at the head of the penis.

AMY: Sure. Can you hear me?

TONTO: Loud and clear.

AMY: Can you help me?

TONTO: How can I do that?

AMY: Rebecca has trapped me inside this thing and won't let me go!

REBECCA: Don't believe a word of it.

> *Rebecca takes a derringer out of her pocket.*

TONTO: Won't let you go. But that means . . .

AMY: Will you please help me?

TONTO: . . . that you're not an animal.

> *Rebecca holds the derringer in front of Tonto's face.*

REBECCA: Took you a while, Tonto, but you figured it out. Get up nice and slow. *(Tonto stands)* Arms up. Come on! Higher!

> *Tonto raises his arms. Rebecca takes her own gun off him and puts it in her holster. Then she takes Tonto's gun and knife and puts them inside her belt.*

TONTO: You won't get far.

REBECCA: You want to bet?

AMY: You have to stop her, Tonto!

REBECCA: Shut up, you! Get some rope.

> *Tonto takes the coiled rope off the saddle.*

Put a loop over her head. And make it snappy.

TONTO: You bad woman.

REBECCA: Skip the sermon.

> *Tonto loops the rope around the neck of the penis.*

REBECCA: Pull it tighter.

> *He pulls it but not very much. Rebecca yanks hard on the rope.*

AMY: That hurts!

TONTO: You shouldn't pull it so tight —

RANGER: Where am I?

REBECCA: What did he say?

TONTO: Him talk in his sleep. Do it all the time.

RANGER: I asked you a question, Tonto. *(he sits up)* Didn't you hear me?

TONTO: I heard you, Kimosabee. *(to Rebecca)* I should go help him.

REBECCA: Stay right where you are.

> *The Ranger stands.*

RANGER: We have to get going. We have a long ride ahead of us today.

TONTO: We sure do, Kimosabee.

> *The Lone Ranger walks to them and stands beside the penis. Rebecca covers them with the derringer.*

RANGER: You ready, Silver?

> *The Ranger puts his leg over the penis and sits on its back.*

AMY: What's he doing on me?

RANGER: That's a good fella. A good horse.

> *The Ranger pats the penis on the side, like one would with a horse.*

AMY: Tell him to get off me!

REBECCA: Shut up.

RANGER: I met a woman, who wore a long silk dress, walking along the road in her bare feet. I couldn't see her face because it was hidden by a beautiful blue shawl. So I leaned out of my saddle and asked where she was going and she said, I'm walking where I have to walk.

AMY: He's heavy!

RANGER: Then I asked her if I could help her and she said, those who need help shouldn't be helped, and she still wouldn't look my way. So I asked, do you know who I am?

AMY: He should go on a diet!

> *Amy rolls the Ranger from side to side.*

RANGER: Easy there, boy. And the woman answered, I know what I am, so I know what you are, and then she looked at me and her face was the most beautiful face I've ever seen and in her eyes I could see myself leaning in my saddle, the road, the hills, the desert, the blue sky, I could see everything around us in her eyes. Then she closed them and stuck out her tongue and on it was a silver bullet.

> *Amy is moving around a lot more and it is difficult for the Ranger to stay on.*

Whoa, boy! So I picked up the bullet and written on it was the word, alias. And she said, plant this and see what will grow.

> *Amy dips down suddenly and then quickly raises herself, bucking the Ranger off the penis. He falls against Rebecca who falls to the ground with him. Tonto jumps onto Rebecca and they wrestle for the gun, which goes off loudly. Amy screams. The Ranger wakes up.*

What's going on?

> *Tonto wins the struggle and takes the derringer and the gun away from Rebecca. He kneels beside Rebecca, covering her with the gun.*

TONTO: Now don't make any false moves.

REBECCA: You're lucky, injun. You're really lucky.

RANGER: *(pointing at the penis)* What the hell?

AMY: My name's Amy. Pleased to meet you.

> *Amy offers her hand to the Ranger. They shake.*

RANGER: I must be dreaming this . . .

TONTO: Afraid not. And as for her . . .

REBECCA: What about me?

AMY: Can you get me out of this, please?

Tonto takes his knife from Rebecca.

TONTO: Where should I cut?

AMY: Along the belly.

Tonto kneels under the penis and cuts the costume.

REBECCA: Don't you cut it up too bad. That's my property.

TONTO: Just sit tight, coyote.

Tonto, finished cutting, helps Amy pull her arms and head from inside the costume. She's dressed in a cowboy shirt which has the sleeves cut off and a skirt which has been tied up around her her hips. Amy stands, stepping out of the costume completely.

AMY: I can breathe again. I can move again. I can see everything! I can see the stars! Up in the sky! How are you up there? I can see you!

REBECCA: She's gone loco.

AMY: No thanks to you.

Amy walks, unsteadily, to Rebecca.

I ought to strangle you. I ought to put my bare hands around your neck and choke you.

REBECCA: Before you do that, maybe you should roll down your skirt.

Amy undoes the knot holding up her skirt. It falls to her ankles.

AMY: You're a no-good skunk, tricking me like that.

Amy puts her hands around Rebecca's neck and then she faints. The Ranger catches her.

RANGER: She's exhausted.

TONTO: Probably hasn't eaten for a couple days.

REBECCA: Amy always eats. Costs me a fortune to feed her.

TONTO: Well, she won't cost you anymore.

Tonto picks up the canteen.

REBECCA: I raised her from an orphan child. I clothed her, tried to teach her reading and writing, treated her like my own flesh and blood.

Tonto presses the canteen to Amy's lips.

RANGER: If this is how you treat your own kind.

REBECCA: It was her idea. She said it would draw more customers into the saloon. Then she got bored and ran off into the desert.

TONTO: She's coming around.

Amy opens her eyes.

RANGER: You fainted.

AMY: I'll say I did. The world started to turn faster and faster on me.

RANGER: You hungry?

AMY: Like a bear.

The Ranger goes to the saddlebags.

Thanks, Tonto.

TONTO: For what?

AMY: For saving me.

Amy puts her arms around Tonto and kisses him. The Ranger brings back a saddlebag.

TONTO: I have to stand up.

AMY: *(she lets go of him)* All right.

Tonto stands and slowly walks downstage.

RANGER: There isn't much food, Amy.

AMY: That's all right.

Amy takes an apple out of the saddlebag. Rebecca picks up the penis costume and examines it. The Ranger walks down to Tonto.

RANGER: What's up?

TONTO: Nothing.

RANGER: You did some pretty fancy work.

TONTO: Thanks.

RANGER: I don't know how I slept through it all.

REBECCA: Can I have a bite?

AMY: Uh unh.

REBECCA: I'm really hungry.

AMY: Find your own food.

Amy pulls the saddlebag out of Rebecca's reach.

RANGER: You know. I've been thinking things over . . . and . . . well, I'm kind of tired.

TONTO: Yeah.

RANGER: I mean, I'm tired of chasing outlaws.

TONTO: We all get fed up, Kimosabee. It's only natural.

RANGER: Somehow it seems like a waste. Maybe it's all been a waste.

TONTO: You're not serious?

RANGER: I think so.

AMY: Hey, Tonto!

TONTO: You can't mean that, Kimosabee.

AMY: Yoo-hoo! Tonto!

TONTO: What do you want?

AMY: I only wanted to say hello. You know, I think you're cute.

TONTO: Thanks a lot.

> *Amy takes a bag of cookies out of the saddlebag. Rebecca takes out her pipe.*

RANGER: I don't think we should go to the Wasteland right now.

TONTO: You're pulling my leg.

RANGER: It can wait a while.

TONTO: But we need silver for your bullets.

RANGER: Not really.

TONTO: And we need bullets to catch outlaws.

RANGER: Who says I want to do that anymore?

> *The Ranger walks away from him.*

TONTO: Who says . . . but what will we do then?

RANGER: I don't know.

TONTO: That's what we've always done.

> *In the following dialogue sequence, the two women talk simultaneously with Tonto and the Ranger.*

REBECCA: *(to Amy)* Well, I think I can fix it.

AMY: Who will you put in it next?

REBECCA: Carol will do.

AMY: She's too fat!

REBECCA: She's hefty, not fat.

AMY: She's a tubby cow if you ask me.

REBECCA: Well, I'm not asking you. Give me a cookie.

AMY: Please.

REBECCA: All right. Please give me a cookie.

> *Amy tosses Rebecca a cookie.*

RANGER: Maybe we can do something different.

TONTO: You can't be serious, Kimosabee.

RANGER: Don't ever call me that.

TONTO: You have gone loco.

RANGER: Not anymore.

TONTO: *(going to him)* Then what should I call you?

RANGER: Alias.

TONTO: Alias?

RANGER: Yeah. That will do for right now. What do you want to be called?

TONTO: Tonto's good enough.

RANGER: Think of something else.

TONTO: But I can't!

RANGER: You have to!

> *Tonto grabs the Ranger's shirt and shakes him.*

TONTO: What's the matter with you? Why are you saying these things? I don't understand, Kimosabee!

RANGER: It's Alias!

TONTO: Why can't we go to Wasteland?

RANGER: Let go of me, Tonto!

TONTO: No, I won't!

RANGER: I want you to let go of me!

> *Tonto stops shaking the Ranger and then lets go of his shirt. Long pause.*

I don't know. It just feels right. That's all. I'm tired of being in the spotlight. Of feeling responsible . . . I don't know . . . it's all mixed up right now . . . but you don't have to come with me, if you don't want to.

TONTO: I think it over.

> *Pause. The Ranger goes to the women.*

AMY: You want a cookie?

RANGER: No thanks. Where's the nearest town?

REBECCA: About five miles.

RANGER: Does it have a saloon?

REBECCA: I own the best saloon this side of the Rockies.

RANGER: Will you buy me a drink there in the morning?

REBECCA: You bet I will.

RANGER: Goodnight, ladies.

REBECCA: Goodnight.

> *Pause. The Ranger goes to the boulder and sits against it.*

AMY: Do you want a cookie, Tonto?

> *Pause.*

They're oatmeal and raisin.

TONTO: What?

AMY: You want a cookie?

TONTO: No thanks.

Pause. Tonto walks up to the Lone Ranger.

Hey . . . Alias.

RANGER: What?

TONTO: I didn't mean to grab you.

RANGER: It's okay.

TONTO: My mother used to call me Thunderbird when I was small.

RANGER: Sounds good to me.

TONTO: All right. Then that's my name now.

AMY: Look at all them stars.

REBECCA: You see the Big Dipper?

AMY: Which one is that?

Tonto and the Lone Ranger shake hands.

REBECCA: You see that group of stars? Well, you have to imagine lines joining them together and all those lines forming a dipper.

AMY: I don't see it.

REBECCA: Can you see the Little Dipper?

AMY: Yeah. But I can't see the other one. Not for the life of me . . .

Tonto walks to the women. The Ranger pulls his hat down on his head and goes to sleep.

Tonto.

TONTO: Call me Thunderbird.

AMY: Will you show me the Big Dipper?

He kneels beside her and points up in the sky. She leans next to him, putting her cheek against his.

TONTO: See where my finger points?

AMY: Yeah. It really does look like a dipper, doesn't it?

REBECCA: Sure it does.

AMY: I'll be damned.

Pause. Amy kisses Tonto on the cheek.

What's the matter?

TONTO: Nothing.

AMY: You look sad.

TONTO: No, I don't.

AMY: Can't I cheer you up?

TONTO: Let's go to sleep.

Tonto sits on the saddle. Amy follows him to the saddle.

AMY: Can you tell me a story?

TONTO: What kind of story?

AMY: I don't know. A legend or something.

TONTO: I think we should sleep.

AMY: Tell me a legend from long ago.

REBECCA: How about it, Thunderbird?

TONTO: Well . . . okay.

> *Pause. Tonto sits back against the saddle. Amy leans over the back of it. Rebecca sits near them.*

When world first began there were no stars in sky and it all black except for moon.

AMY: That must have been scarey.

TONTO: It was. And it made moon feel lonely and so he cry a lot. So great mother bear decide to visit moon and cheer him up. When she was halfway there, her cubs got hungry so she had to stop and feed them.

> *Rebecca lies down on her back. She's still listening to the story.*

But there was this one cub, who kept sucking on her tit and wouldn't let go. He was very strong for his age and when she pulled away from him, she did it too fast and milk spread all over the sky. And then it change into star over there. And star here. And soon there were millions of stars. And stars talk and laugh with moon and so he wasn't lonely anymore and that's the end.

> *Tonto looks at Rebecca who has gone to sleep. Amy has gone to sleep too. She has her hand on Tonto's shoulder.*

TONTO: I'll go with Kimosabee into town tomorrow. I'll go . . . cause I ride with him. Sooner or later we'll go to Wasteland and get silver for bullets. Sooner or later we'll go. We'll have to.

> *Tonto slides down until his head rests against the saddle. He closes his eyes. The lights fade to black.*

underground

102

To Bob Dolhanty and Ken Gass.

CHARACTERS

AL, twenty-three

CLAIRE, thirty

GERRY, twenty-nine

There's nothing artificial about this room, it has the look of being lived in. In the centre there is a small wooden table and a chair. On the table there is an alarm clock. There is a comfortable sofa in the left corner of the room. Beside the sofa is a stand-up lamp. There is also the hall doorway which leads to the bedroom and bathroom. Beside this doorway is a framed photograph of two people.

On the other side of the room there are: an easy chair, a small bookcase with paperbacks and magazines, and a doorway which leads to the kitchen and the front door.

In the centre of the back wall there is a poster. In it are three people in dramatic profile, who look defiantly towards the right. The black man has his fists raised in the air. Next to him is a young man with a straw hat, who holds a rifle. Then a young Chinese woman, her hair blowing in the wind. The caption above them says in four languages (Chinese, English, French, Spanish): Support the Anti-Imperialist Struggle of the People of the World.

UNDERGROUND was first produced at the Factory Theatre Lab, Toronto, in 1975, with the following cast:

CLAIRE	Samantha Langevin
AL	Jim Henshaw
GERRY	Nick Mancuso

Directed by Eric Steiner

UNDERGROUND

Act One

Complete darkness. It is quiet enough to hear the ticking of the alarm clock. A few notes from a trumpet can be heard from the bedroom. The hall light is turned on and a block of light spills onto the living room floor.

Claire walks down the hall and stops in the doorway. She wears a silk dressing gown. She goes to the lamp and turns on the light. She has a hairbrush in her hand and surveys the room. A few more notes come from the bedroom. The clock reads five o'clock in the afternoon. Claire idly brushes her hair.

A few more notes come from the bedroom. Claire stops brushing and looks in the direction of the hall doorway and then there is one long blast of the trumpet. Claire goes to the sofa, which is covered in books and magazines, throws a couple on the floor, and sits down. She brushes her hair again.

Al walks down the hall and stops in the doorway. He wears work clothes and work boots. He has a toy trumpet with three keys. He watches Claire.

AL: Well. What's the answer?

CLAIRE: The answer to what?

AL: To the question I asked you.

CLAIRE: You asked me a lot of questions in the bedroom. Which one was it?

AL: You know which one it was.

CLAIRE: No, I'm afraid I don't.

AL: Come on. Stop kidding around.

CLAIRE: I'm not.

AL: Sure you are. You're always kidding me.

CLAIRE: Well, I'm not this time.
          Pause.

AL: I asked you, how often does he come?

CLAIRE: I answered that one already.

AL: No, you didn't.

CLAIRE: You sure?

AL: I'm positive.

CLAIRE: I guess he comes as often as he wants.

AL: So you just let him come and go as he pleases?

CLAIRE: I don't have much say in what he does. You know that.

AL: No, I don't.

CLAIRE: I already told you, Al.

AL: Then tell me again.

CLAIRE: Maybe I don't feel like it.

AL: What do you feel like?

>*Pause. Al approaches the sofa and stands in front of her.*

Huh? What do you feel like tonight?

>*Pause.*

CLAIRE: You wouldn't understand.

AL: And how do you know that?

CLAIRE: Because I do.

AL: Are you saying I'm too stupid to understand your problem?

CLAIRE: Of course not.

AL: Is that what you're saying?

CLAIRE: Of course it isn't.

>*Pause. Al moves to the table. Claire picks up an alarm clock which was wedged between the two pillows of the sofa. It isn't running. She winds it up.*

AL: So. You let him come and go as he pleases.

CLAIRE: It's a free country.

AL: That's right. This is a free country. You can move around if you feel like it. You can quit your job if you're not happy. You can always find another job somewhere else. They're crying out for workers all across the country. My foreman said he could use ten more workers like me. Just think about that. Ten more workers like me. So if I want to go to a new city or town, all I have to do is pack my bags and leave. That's all I have to do. There won't be any forms to fill out. There won't be any questions. There won't be any inter- rogations.

CLAIRE: I should hope not.

AL: No one would allow themselves to be interrogated.

>*Pause. Claire sets the alarm off on the clock. They both let it ring until it stops.*

What did you do that for?

CLAIRE: Because I felt like it.

AL: I hate those noisy things. I hate them more than anything in the world.

CLAIRE: They're not that bad, you know.

AL: You don't have to get up every morning with one ringing in your ears.

CLAIRE: I get up every morning and it doesn't bother me.

AL: What do you mean? You don't get up before noon.

CLAIRE: I wake up before that.

AL: But you don't get out of bed before noon. Do you?

CLAIRE: Well, I usually wake up around eleven.

AL: I have to get up early. I have to get up when it's still dark outside. I have to go piss in the toilet. I have to put toothpaste on my brush and clean my teeth. I have to wash my face. I have to put shaving cream on my face and shave. I have to spray deodorant on my armpits. I have to brush my hair. Then I have to get dressed. My shirt. My pants. My socks. My work boots. And if I have time, I have a cup of coffee and some toast with honey or peanut butter.

CLAIRE: I like honey.

AL: Do you?

CLAIRE: I love it. I put it on everything I can. In my cereal, on my toast, in my tea. I don't know what I'd do without honey.

AL: I've never seen you use it.

CLAIRE: You haven't?

> *Al shakes his head.*

Well, I do. I use it quite frequently.

AL.:   I just use it when I have the time.

CLAIRE: So you're in a rush in the mornings?

AL: You could say that.

> *Pause. Al sits in the chair by the table. He puts the trumpet on the table.*

Do you support the anti-imperialist struggle of the people of the world?

CLAIRE: Pardon?

AL: I asked you if you supported the anti-imperialist struggle —

CLAIRE: You know. I wouldn't like getting up when it's dark outside.

AL: I don't think anyone does.

CLAIRE: I really don't see how anyone could.

AL: I know I don't. It's dark when I go to work and I come home. It's dark when I go to sleep and when I wake up.

CLAIRE: But in the summer.

AL: Now that's different. In the summer there's light all the time.

CLAIRE: That must be nice.

AL: It's a change all right.

CLAIRE: I like summer evenings the best. I like them just at dusk when the light makes everything so soft, as if everything was in a painting. I always walk somewhere I've never been before, so I can pretend I'm discovering something new, as if I was an explorer from a distant star. Claire, I tell myself, you have to look at all these houses, apartment blocks, supermarkets, parking lots, gas stations and cars, as if they were brand new. Sometimes it works and I can look at them that way. But most of the time I just shake my head and ask myself, why do they do it? What makes them go through with all this?

AL: I've never seen you walking around.

CLAIRE: That's impossible. I go whenever I can.

AL: I've never seen you.

> *Pause. Claire takes out a cigarette. Al goes to her and lights it with his lighter. Then he stands in front of the framed photograph on the wall.*

I remember where this was taken. It was that weekend we stayed at the beach. The hotel was all right, although the room service was lousy. From our windows you could see the beach and the sea. I remember how we used to lie in bed and listen to the waves roll up and down on the sand. All night long. Up and down that beach. I thought those waves would get tired of doing the same thing all the time. But they didn't, did they?

CLAIRE: That's not you in the photograph.

AL: What do you mean?

CLAIRE: I've never had my picture taken with you.

AL: What are you talking about?

CLAIRE: I never have and I never will.

> *Al stands in front of Claire.*

AL: I have hundreds of photos of you and me. Hundreds of them.

CLAIRE: That's what you say.

AL: You can look at them if you want.

CLAIRE: Well, I don't.

AL: One's of us suntanning on the beach.

CLAIRE: I never suntanned with you.

AL: One's of us swimming in the ocean.

CLAIRE: I never swam with you.

AL: Sure you did.

CLAIRE: You're wrong, Al.

AL: You haven't forgotten the crawl, have you?

CLAIRE: Sorry.

AL: How about the breaststroke?

> *Claire shakes her head.*

The butterfly?

She shakes her head again.

Treading water?

CLAIRE: I can't swim.

AL: I taught you how.

CLAIRE: You never taught me anything.

Pause. Al sits beside her.

AL: It was our holiday together.

CLAIRE: There was no holiday.

AL: That's when we got away from it all.

CLAIRE: Maybe you did.

AL: You had the time of your life there. You said so yourself. You kept telling me how much fun you were having.

CLAIRE: I never went anywhere with you.

AL: There was dancing every night on the patio. There was a really good rock and roll band knocking the music out. That drummer smashed the shit out of his drums. I don't know how they took all that punishment. And the guitar player. The lead guitar player who thought he was Mick Jagger and Jimmy Page combined. He was the worst part of the band. If they got a new lead, they might go somewhere. That's what I said to myself. Get a new lead and you'll be really cooking.

Pause. Claire goes to the table. She picks up a magazine and flips through it.

But you couldn't get enough of their sound. You really can shake it up on the dance floor. I never told you this before but when you want to move it, you can really move it. I think the lead guitarist wanted to give it to you. I think he wanted to fuck you. I bet you knew he wanted to screw you. I bet you knew all the time.

Pause. Claire sits on the chair beside the table. She butts her cigarette and continues to flip through the magazine.

CLAIRE: I never danced with you.

AL: You used to boogie with me every night underneath the stars.

CLAIRE: I can't dance.

AL: That's what you say. I've seen you move. I've seen all the guys looking at you. They like the way you move.

CLAIRE: Good for them.

AL: That lead guitarist wanted to give it to you.

CLAIRE: Is that so?

AL: That's right.

CLAIRE: How did you know?

AL: I could tell.

CLAIRE: How could you tell?

AL: The way he was looking at you.

CLAIRE: How was he looking at me?

AL: He was making very suggestive movements.

CLAIRE: Such as?

AL: With his hips. With his guitar. And with his mouth.

CLAIRE: With his mouth?

AL: He was doing this with his tongue.

> *Pause. Al sticks out his tongue and makes licking motions with it. Claire watches him.*

CLAIRE: I don't see anything wrong with that.

AL: You don't?

CLAIRE: This is a free country. People can stick their tongues out of their mouths if they want.

AL: I know, but it was the way he moved it.

CLAIRE: People can move their tongues any way they want to.

AL: It meant he wanted to screw you.

CLAIRE: Well, maybe he did.

AL: What's that?

CLAIRE: I said maybe he did.

AL: *(he stands)* Maybe he did what?

CLAIRE: Maybe he did screw me.

AL: *(he approaches her)* And when did this happen?

CLAIRE: At the end of one of their sets.

> *Al stands beside her now.*

AL: Where was I?

CLAIRE: I don't know.

AL: You never told me about this before.

CLAIRE: You never asked me.

> *Pause.*

AL: Was it any good?

CLAIRE: He was no Mick Jagger, that's for sure.

> *Pause. Al moves around the table and stops when he's opposite her. She continues to flip through the magazine.*

AL: So when's he getting here?

CLAIRE: When he gets here, I guess.

AL: You don't know?

CLAIRE: No, I don't.

AL: No special time?

CLAIRE: No.

AL: Ten?

> *Claire shakes her head.*

Eleven?

> *She shakes her head again.*

Eleven-thirty?

CLAIRE: He'll get here when he comes.

AL: How come him and I have never met?

CLAIRE: I don't know.

AL: You'd think him and I would have met by now.

CLAIRE: I've never thought about it.

AL: You wouldn't. It's just like you not to think about something like that.

> *Pause. Al plays a few notes on the trumpet.*
>
> *Claire doesn't respond and continues to flip through the magazine. Al tries again, this time he plays the three keys in sequence, holding each note the same length of time. He walks around the table and when he goes past her, he leans over and directs the sound at her. But Claire doesn't look at him.*
>
> *Al goes around the table again. Then she picks up the alarm clock and winds up the alarm on it. Al stops beside her and directs the sound of the trumpet at her. Claire is about to release the alarm when Al takes the trumpet from his mouth.*

AL: I can stop playing if you want.

CLAIRE: You don't have to stop.

AL: I don't?

CLAIRE: Why should you? You sounded fine.

AL: I wasn't too loud?

CLAIRE: Not at all.

AL: I just thought.

CLAIRE: You thought what?

AL: Nothing.

CLAIRE: *(she holds up the clock)* About this? *(pause)* I was winding it up. Clocks run down and have to be wound up again, so they'll keep the right time. You didn't have to worry about me —

AL: I wasn't worried about that. I wouldn't worry about something as unimportant as that.

CLAIRE: It seemed to me you were —

AL: There you go again, telling me what I was doing. Everyone is always telling me what I'm doing. Or what I'm thinking. You always seem to know all the answers before I do.

CLAIRE: You don't have to get like that.

AL: Get like what?

CLAIRE: You know what I mean.

AL: Maybe I don't know what you mean. Maybe you should try spelling it out for someone as stupid as me.

CLAIRE: I didn't say you were stupid.

AL: You don't have to say it, Claire.

> *Pause. She knows better than to answer. Al, with the trumpet in his hand, sits on the arm of the sofa.*

What are you going to do when he comes?

CLAIRE: I don't know.

AL: What are you going to talk about?

CLAIRE: How am I supposed to know that?

AL: You have to talk about something. We all have to talk about something. I mean, you can't just sit there and not say anything.

CLAIRE: Some people can.

AL: What do you mean by that?

CLAIRE: Nothing.

AL: I suppose you think I talk too much. I suppose you think I never keep my mouth shut. It's true that I like to talk. I just have a gift for words. It doesn't matter what I do, I always seem to find the right word. It's nice having a gift like that. Some people have it, while others don't.

> *Al goes and sits in the easy chair.*

Does he like to talk?

CLAIRE: Sometimes he does.

AL: What does he talk about?

CLAIRE: What he wants to.

AL: How about politics?

CLAIRE: No.

AL: What does he think about the anti-imperialist struggle?

CLAIRE: I don't know.

AL: He must have some opinion.

CLAIRE: If he does, he never told me.

AL: I mean, you're either with it or you're against it.

CLAIRE: I guess so.

Pause.

AL: It all sounds pretty boring to me.

CLAIRE: It isn't for me. You have to be here to understand what happens when he's in the room.

AL: What happens?

CLAIRE: I can't put it into words.

AL: You can try.

CLAIRE: I would if it was possible.

AL: You just don't want to, that's all. *(pause)* All right. You and him have talked about what you want to talk about. What will you do then?

CLAIRE: I really couldn't tell you.

AL: Will you play some games?

CLAIRE: Maybe.

AL: Some gin rummy?

CLAIRE: Maybe.

AL: Some ping pong?

CLAIRE: Maybe.

AL: Some snakes and ladders?

CLAIRE: Maybe.

AL: Some kissing? *(pause)* Does he like to kiss?

CLAIRE: Sometimes.

AL: Where does he like to kiss you?

CLAIRE: On the mouth usually.

AL: How about your neck?

CLAIRE: Sometimes he does.

AL: How about your arms?

CLAIRE: Once in a while.

AL: Your shoulders?

CLAIRE: Yes, he likes them.

AL: Well, he should. You have nice ones. Some girls don't have nice ones at all. Some have really square shoulders. Yours are rounded, very well rounded.

CLAIRE: I never noticed.

AL: Most people never notice anything good about themselves. They just remember all the bad points.

CLAIRE: Do you do that?

AL: Do I do what?

CLAIRE: Not notice your good points.

AL: I never really thought about it.

CLAIRE: Because you do have your good points.

AL: How many do you think I have?

CLAIRE: You have your share.

AL: How many is that?

CLAIRE: It's enough.

AL: Do you think it's more than average?

CLAIRE: You don't want to get greedy about it, now do you?

                Pause.

AL: Does he undress you?

CLAIRE: Sometimes he does.

AL: Or is it better when you undress yourself and he watches?

CLAIRE: Sometimes it is.

AL: What do you take off first?

CLAIRE: My blouse.

AL: Then what's next?

CLAIRE: My skirt.

AL: Then what?

CLAIRE: My stockings.

AL: What about your shoes?

CLAIRE: What about them?

AL: Don't you take them off before your stockings?

CLAIRE: Of course I do.

AL: I guess your panties must be next.

CLAIRE: That's right.

AL: Then you must lie down on the bed.

CLAIRE: No, I don't.

AL: What do you do then?

CLAIRE: I help undress him.

AL: So he likes being undressed?

CLAIRE: He loves it.

AL: Does he help?

CLAIRE: I do everything for him. He just stands and watches me undress him. I unbutton his shirt and take that off. I untie his shoelaces and take off his shoes and socks. Then I unbutton his pants and slide them down his legs. He steps out of them and then I —

AL: He just stands there while you do this? He doesn't say anything?

CLAIRE: What should he say?

AL: Does he tell you how much he loves you?

CLAIRE: He doesn't have to tell me that.

AL: So you don't believe in it?

CLAIRE: Well, I don't make him say something he doesn't want to.

AL: So he doesn't believe in it?

CLAIRE: I don't know.

AL: You never ask him?

CLAIRE: I never thought about it before.

> *Pause. He gets up and approaches her.*

AL: Then what?

CLAIRE: Then we kiss each other.

AL: And after that?

CLAIRE: We run our hands over each other's bodies.

AL: And where does he run his?

CLAIRE: All over.

AL: Over your breasts?

CLAIRE: Yes.

AL: Over your thighs?

CLAIRE: Yes.

AL: Your shoulders?

> *She nods her head.*

Your belly?

> *She nods her head.*

Through your hair?

> *She nods her head.*

And what do you do?

> *He stands close to her, looking down at her.*

CLAIRE: I run my hands over his body.

AL: All over?

CLAIRE: Wherever I want.

AL: Then what?

CLAIRE: We lie down. We hold each other in our arms. We kiss each other on the mouth. We touch each other with our tongues. We kiss on the neck, on the shoulders, on the arms. He kisses my right breast and then my left breast.

AL: Do you like that?

CLAIRE: I like it very much. I like everything he does. I like his confidence. He knows what I want and he knows how to satisfy. He knows I like him to whisper in my ear.

AL: He whispers in your ear?

CLAIRE: That's right.

AL: What does he say?

CLAIRE: Whatever he feels like.

AL: What does he usually say?

CLAIRE: I don't know.

AL: You must remember.

CLAIRE: I just know that whatever it is, I like it.

She stands and goes to the sofa.

AL: Where are you going?

CLAIRE: To get a smoke, if it's all right with you.

She takes out a cigarette.

Do you have a light?

AL: Are you sure you can't remember?

CLAIRE: I thought you had a lighter.

AL: You must be able to remember something.

CLAIRE: Do you have matches?

AL: One word. One sentence. That's all I want.

CLAIRE: Don't you have anything?

AL: Don't I have what?

CLAIRE: A lighter. A match.

He takes out his lighter and lights her cigarette.

Would you like a beer?

AL: No thanks.

CLAIRE: They're nice and cold.

AL: Not right now.

CLAIRE: They'd quench your thirst.

Pause. He shakes his head and sits on the arm of the sofa.

I don't know if I'd like one or not. I don't usually drink much, although I like the occasional drink in the bar. I don't mind that at all, having a drink with a few friends. But I don't make a habit of it. You won't find me down there every night like some people. That's what really scares me. When I go in a bar I haven't been in for a couple of weeks and I see the same people drinking at the same tables. And you know they've been down there every night. It's almost as if two weeks haven't passed except you know that they have. But there's something even scarier about bars. All these people crowd together in one room, sit on top of each other, drinking beer and smoking cigarettes, and try to talk through all the noise, all the screaming, all the beer glasses, all the music from the juke box. All these people are having a good time. But they can't do it by themselves. You never hear someone say he had a good time by himself. Do you?

AL: No, I don't think I have.

CLAIRE: I never have either.

> *She goes to the table and sits on top of it. She rests her feet on the chair.*

Do you like to drink much?

AL: Sometimes I do.

CLAIRE: When?

AL: When I feel like getting loaded.

> *Pause. She crosses her legs.*

CLAIRE: You don't have to worry, you know.

AL: I'm not worried.

CLAIRE: You look like you are.

AL: I may look like it but I don't feel like it.

CLAIRE: All right. But you won't have to worry with me taking care of you.

AL: No, I guess I won't.

CLAIRE: Because I'm one of the best there is.

AL: I'm sure you're very good.

CLAIRE: *(laughs at this)* Some people have said that around here.

AL: Does Gerry say that?

> *She suddenly stops laughing.*

Is that what he says to you?

CLAIRE: You know. You can whisper something to me, if you want.

AL: You wouldn't mind?

> *She shakes her head.*

You sure?

CLAIRE: Of course I'm sure. Come here.

> *Pause. Al approaches the table. He stops about a foot away from her.*

You'll have to get closer than that.

> *Pause. He leans near her. She puts her arm around his shoulders and pulls him closer.*

You can start whenever you want.

Pause. He whispers into her ear. We see his lips move but we can't hear any specific words. He stops but she keeps her arm around his waist.

CLAIRE: Is that it?

AL: That's it.

CLAIRE: That was only three words.

AL: I thought they'd be enough.

CLAIRE: There must be more.

Pause. She pulls him close again. Al whispers but this time he repeats himself, mouthing three words over and over again. Finally he stops.

AL: How did you like that?

CLAIRE: I liked it very much. *(she hugs him)* You didn't have anything to worry about.

AL: I wasn't worried about it. It never even crossed my mind that you might not like it. What made you think I was worried?

CLAIRE: I didn't think you were, Al. It was —

AL: Then what did you say that for?

CLAIRE: It's a figure of speech. It's something you say when . . .

AL: When what?

CLAIRE: When you can't think of anything else to say.

AL: You mean you didn't like it?

CLAIRE: I liked it.

Al breaks away from her.

AL: You're just saying that. You're just making it all up. You know you didn't enjoy it.

CLAIRE: I enjoyed it.

AL: You know it can't compare to what Gerry can tell you. You're just trying to protect me. You're trying to say what you think I want you to say. You don't think I'm interested in the truth. Well, I'm not like other people. I'm not afraid of the truth. I never have and I never will be. I don't need protection from anyone. I want you to understand that right now.

CLAIRE: I understand perfectly.

AL: I bet you do. I bet you understand what I've said. You can't understand it. No one can. We all go through these motions. We all make these sounds . . . these noises.

Suddenly there is the piercing sound of a jet above them, which seems close enough to hit the house. It passes from left to right and fades as quickly as it came.

CLAIRE: He was flying low!

AL: They shouldn't be allowed so close to the ground. There should be a law. They don't have any right to come this close. He could have crashed and killed us!

CLAIRE: But he didn't.

AL: He could have easily made a mistake and crashed into the house.

CLAIRE: You know, they sound closer than they really are. They're really quite high up.

AL: Even if they are, I still don't like them.

CLAIRE: Ever been up in one?

AL: Nope.

CLAIRE: Ever going on one?

AL: Not if I can help it.

CLAIRE: How come? I've been up a thousand times.

AL: Good for you. I like trains a lot more.

CLAIRE: They drive me crazy.

AL: I like trains. I like everything about them. I like the trains that run underground. They're fast and efficient. They take people where they want to go. There's no fuss, no traffic jams. There's nothing to worry about. You get on, you ride to where you want and then you get off.

CLAIRE: I never go underground.

AL: You should. It would save you time. Which reminds me. I was waiting on the platform to catch the subway over here. I was just standing there, minding my own business, looking at the advertisements, when this young guy runs past me. I didn't pay any attention to him. He looked like any other guy you see in the subway every day. Except he seemed to be in a hurry. He was standing right on the edge of the platform, looking down in the tunnel. Then the wind started to blow and grab at your jacket and your pants, so you knew a train was coming. The rumbling kept getting louder and louder and then you could see the light reflected in the curve of the tunnel. A few seconds later the train came speeding around the curve with the driver in the front. *(he pauses)* So there I was, with my hands in my pockets, watching the train come around the curve. And not for one moment did it ever cross my mind that anything could happen. You never even consider things like that. So here's the train rushing like a bullet up the tracks and here's the guy standing on the edge of the platform. Then all of a sudden, he jumps down between the tracks. And what does he do? He stands there, looking at the train coming at him, looking at the driver in his cab. *(he pauses)* It was only a second before the train ran into him and dragged him up the tracks to the end of the platform. The train hit him before the driver even made a move for the brakes.

Pause.

CLAIRE: It must have been terrible to watch.

AL: Some people went to the end of the platform to see the body. Some got on the train and sat down. They tried to pretend as if nothing had happened.

CLAIRE: What did you do?

AL: I walked to the end of the platform. His body was covered with a raincoat which had a rolled newspaper in its pocket. His hand was near the paper, almost as if he was about to pull it out and read it.

CLAIRE: There's one problem when things like that happen. You always say to yourself if I had only known, I could have done something.

AL: But that would mean being able to see into the future.

CLAIRE: And what's wrong with that? If you could do that, you would have known what was going to happen. Then you could have talked to him and listened to his problems.

AL: Maybe so.

CLAIRE: That's all these people need, you know.

AL: I don't know. Things could have been pretty bad for him.

CLAIRE: I doubt it. They always magnify everything.

AL: Maybe he was broke.

Al sits on the arm of the sofa.

CLAIRE: He could have found a job.

AL: Maybe he was hungry.

CLAIRE: Don't be ridiculous. No one goes hungry in this country.

AL: Maybe he was in love with a woman and she didn't want him anymore.

CLAIRE: Maybe she did. Maybe she had to tell him to get out. That's still no reason for him being so stupid.

AL: What's so stupid about it?

CLAIRE: I don't see anything positive about it.

AL: I've seen people waste their lives in worse ways.

Claire gets down off the table.

CLAIRE: You want to go out?

AL: Where?

CLAIRE: For a drink.

AL: There's beer in the fridge.

CLAIRE: I feel like going out.

AL: You were out last night too.

CLAIRE: That was last night. You coming or not?

AL: All right.

Pause. Claire walks up the hall and into the bedroom. Al gets up and walks to the table. He picks up the trumpet and turns it over in his hands.

(to himself) A guy doesn't give up his life for nothing. That's one thing you can be sure of. And if a guy does something like that, you can't call it stupid. That's just not the right word for it.

CLAIRE: *(off)* What'd you say?

AL: *(to Claire)* I said if you don't hurry up, they'll drink all the booze.

CLAIRE: *(off)* I doubt that.

Al raises the trumpet to his eye and uses it like a telescope.

AL: Too bad this wasn't a telescope which let you see into the past and the future. Too bad I didn't have it when he came onto the platform. I could have looked at him and seen every event in his past and the last event in his future. I don't think it would have made any difference though. I wouldn't have stopped him. I couldn't have. I mean, you just don't go up to someone and say —

Claire walks down the hall and into the living room. She wears a low-cut dress and has a raincoat over her arm. Al is still looking through the trumpet.

CLAIRE: Say what?

AL: *(lowering the trumpet)* I thought you'd be all night.

CLAIRE: What were you going to say?

AL: That we should get going. That is, if we want to get loaded.

He puts the trumpet on the table.

CLAIRE: Now that sounds like a good idea.

Claire walks into the kitchen, opens the front door and goes out. Al turns out the light on the stand-up lamp. Then he goes into the kitchen and turns out its light, shutting the front door after him.

The block of light from the hall spills onto the living room floor. You can hear the ticking of the alarm clocks.

Then the hall light fades to black.

Act Two

Darkness. We hear the two clocks ticking and then the front door is opened and closed. Gerry stands in the kitchen doorway, looking in at the darkness. He turns on the kitchen light. He is dressed in a well-cut three piece suit with a co-ordinated shirt and tie. He has a suitcase in one hand and a portable tape recorder hangs from a strap around his shoulder.

Gerry turns on the lamp and then looks around the room. He is displeased. The sofa is still covered with books and magazines. The table has empty beer bottles and a full ashtray on it. The alarm clock reads ten minutes after nine o'clock.

Gerry clears a space on the table and puts his tape recorder on it. He picks up his suitcase and walks to the poster. He studies it carefully.

GERRY: Support the anti-imperialist struggle of the people of the world.

Gerry goes into the hall, turns on its light and walks into the bedroom. Claire opens the front door, closes it, walks through the kitchen and stands in the doorway. She sees the tape recorder, walks to the table and then takes off her raincoat. She throws it on the easy chair.

CLAIRE: Is that you?

GERRY: *(off)* It's me all right.

CLAIRE: When did you get in?

GERRY: *(off)* Just now.

Claire stuffs some magazines under the pillows of the sofa and she picks up some books and puts them on the bookcase.

CLAIRE: How was the flight?

GERRY: *(off)* Fantastic. Just fantastic. *(pause)* Where were you?

CLAIRE: I was out.

GERRY: *(off)* Out where?

CLAIRE: For a drink.

Pause. Gerry comes down the hall and into the living room. Claire stops tidying.

GERRY: The flight was really fantastic. One of the best I've had in years.

CLAIRE: Are you tired?

GERRY: No.

CLAIRE: You should be after coming all that way.

GERRY: I know I should be. The reason I'm not is that as I was sitting in my seat, drinking my scotch, I looked out my window at the ground thirty-nine thousand feet below. And I started to think about all the time zones we would fly through. Now since we're flying through four time zones, does that mean you're in one time zone or the other? Or do you remain in the one you left until you get to your new zone? Or do you have any real time when you're on a plane? Now if you have no real time on a plane, then you're not growing older. You're staying the same age because you're flying through time.

CLAIRE: Do you want a beer?

GERRY: I'd love one. I hope you're listening to me.

CLAIRE: I am, don't worry.

> *Claire picks up the empty beer bottles on the table and goes into the kitchen. Gerry takes off his jacket and hangs it on the back of the chair.*

> *Claire opens the fridge, gets out the beer and opens it. As Gerry talks, he sets up the recorder for recording. He plugs the microphone in and puts a tape cassette in the recorder.*

GERRY: Now that started me thinking about all the other zones in the world. If there's twenty-four hours in a day, there must be twenty-four time zones. And everyone lives in a zone. People five hours ahead are probably sleeping right now. People eight hours behind us are probably eating their breakfast or going to work. Are you listening to me?

CLAIRE: *(from kitchen)* Sure I am.

GERRY: Everyone moves in their own time zone. People all over the world are eating or loving or dreaming or dying. Someone is dying right now. You could be laughing at a joke and someone else is dying in another time zone. What do you think about that?

> *Pause. Claire is making noise in the kitchen.*

We all go through the same thing day after day. We get up in the morning, we move around in the day, we go to sleep at night. But we all think of ourselves as individuals and what we do as being different.

> *Claire comes back in the living room with two beers. She gives him one.*

And everyone is doing something which will affect me sooner or later, just as what I do will affect them. Everyone is living in my past or my future. *(pause)* Do you see how important it is to understand that?

CLAIRE: It doesn't change anything for me. I still have to live my life.

GERRY: I think it would change things for you. If we could forget the idea that the zone we live in is the only one that matters —

CLAIRE: I forgot to bring in the chips. Do you want some?

GERRY: Not especially.

> *Claire goes into the kitchen. Gerry turns the tape recorder on to record.*

GERRY: *(to himself, as he deals with the problem)* Time seems to have a sequential order. But what happens when someone moves into another time zone and doesn't prepare himself? Then he's living in two zones at once . . .

> *Pause. Claire comes back with a bowl of potato chips. She offers him some but he shakes his head. She picks up her beer from the table and sits on the sofa.*

CLAIRE: A friend came over while you were away.

GERRY: Is that right?

CLAIRE: We went out for a drink today.

GERRY: Did you have a good time?

CLAIRE: Yes, we did.

GERRY: *(he nods at the poster)* Is that his?

CLAIRE: Yes.

GERRY: Does he believe in it?

CLAIRE: I guess he does. I never asked him. But he's the one that put it up on the wall.

GERRY: What's your friend like?

CLAIRE: He's very interesting.

GERRY: In what ways?

He sits on the table, facing her.

CLAIRE: For one thing, he's a good talker. He really likes to do that. He'll talk about anything and everything. For instance, he said, while we were sitting in the bar today, that he'd kill himself if I asked him.

GERRY: He said that.

CLAIRE: *(she smiles)* He really did. And he was so serious when he said it. It was as if the whole world depended on it.

GERRY: Why would he do something like that?

CLAIRE: *(still smiling)* So he could prove how much he loves me.

GERRY: And just how much does he?

CLAIRE: Quite a lot, I guess. I mean, you don't find men saying they'll kill themselves every day. Now do you?

GERRY: No, you don't.

CLAIRE: But other than that, he's quite ordinary. And he can't compare to you. Not many people can though. Every time I meet someone, I compare him to you. Sometimes I say to myself, here's one just as good as Gerry. And then he'll do something stupid.

GERRY: Like what?

CLAIRE: I don't know. Just something stupid.

GERRY: You shouldn't be so critical of people.

CLAIRE: I'm not. I try and get along with them.

GERRY: You start tearing people down as soon as they come into the room. You look them over and say to yourself, I don't like his shirt or his hair. Don't try and deny it either. I've seen you in action. I've seen what you can do to a man once you get going. I bet you really went over this guy.

CLAIRE: I didn't do anything of the kind.

GERRY: That's hard to believe. You probably found something wrong with him as soon as he opened his mouth.

CLAIRE: Well. He never said anything.

GERRY: Your friend was probably polite. Most people don't go out of their way to offend people. Not you though. You enjoy it. You thrive on it. You're addicted to it.

CLAIRE: Don't worry, if I had said something, he would have told me.

GERRY: You can't fool me. Remember that party we went to? Remember what you did to that man? You were with him for fifteen minutes and you had him on his knees, begging you to stop. I couldn't believe it.

CLAIRE: That guy was an asshole.

GERRY: You bring out the worst in a person. I don't know how you do it but you do it every time. Take a perfect stranger. Take any stranger off the street and I bet within half an hour you could bring out the worst in him.

CLAIRE: What do you mean by that?

GERRY: You know what I mean.

Pause.

CLAIRE: That's not true and you know it.

GERRY: I bet you did it with your friend.

He stands.

CLAIRE: I'm afraid you're wrong.

GERRY: What happened then?

CLAIRE: Not much really.

GERRY: Did he make love to you?

Gerry approaches her.

CLAIRE: That's none of your business.

GERRY: Did he try to make love with you?

CLAIRE: I don't have to tell you if I don't want to.

GERRY: I never said you did.

Pause. He stands in front of her now.

How was it?

Pause.

Any good?

Pause.

Did you do it standing up?

Pause.

Or lying down?

Pause.

In the bed?

Pause.

Or on the floor?

Pause. Gerry leans down until he's face to face with Claire.

With the lights on?

Pause.

Or in the dark?

Pause.

What kind of noises did he make?

Pause.

Did he grunt a lot?

Pause. Gerry straightens up.

How much did you sweat?

Pause.

What time did you do it?

CLAIRE: How should I know that?

GERRY: You must have some idea.

CLAIRE: I don't have any idea.

GERRY: I was probably flying while you two were going at it.

> *Pause. Gerry turns and goes back to the table, where he picks up his beer. He takes a long hit from it.*

CLAIRE: Aren't you going to ask any more questions?

Pause.

Don't you want to know?

Pause.

Don't you want to know everything about it?

Pause.

I'll tell you if you sit down. I'll tell you what went on but you'll have to sit down first.

> *Pause. Gerry turns and faces her. He takes another long hit off his beer.*

It wasn't really that good. It wasn't as good as some of the times we've had together. But it gave me something to do. He wasn't bad at it either. He was around average, I guess. Nothing spectacular but quite adequate.

> *Claire pauses deliberately.*

Shall I go on? *(pause)* I won't if you don't want me to.

> *Pause. Claire stands and approaches Gerry.*

He undressed himself. I didn't help him. He undressed on one side of the bed while I undressed on the other. He hung his shirt on a hanger and even folded his pants properly, and hung them up too. I guess he doesn't like them getting creased.

Pause. Gerry moves away from her and goes to the framed photograph on the wall.

So there we were, looking at each other across the bed. We climbed in between the sheets and he put his arms around me and I put my arms around him. He kissed me on the lips and I kissed him back. Shall I go on?

Pause. Gerry turns and faces her.

Do you want me to go on? I can if you want. I don't mind if you want to hear all about it.

GERRY: Where did you get it from?

CLAIRE: Get what?

GERRY: This photograph.

CLAIRE: I've had that ever since I can remember.

GERRY: Well, I've never had my picture taken with you.

She goes to Gerry. She looks at the photograph with pride.

CLAIRE: Of course you have. This was taken when we stayed in that cabin by the lake.

GERRY: I never went to a cabin with you.

CLAIRE: Of course you did. We had the time of our lives there.

GERRY: Maybe you did.

CLAIRE: We'd have breakfast in bed and then we'd smoke and read the newspapers. Or else we'd lie there without doing anything and listen to the waves lap on the shore of the lake.

GERRY: I never stay in bed after I wake up. I always get up right away.

He sits on the chair by the table.

CLAIRE: We went swimming every afternoon. And we raced each other out to the raft in the middle of the lake. But you always beat me. Every time, no matter how much of a lead you gave me, you always beat me.

GERRY: I never swam with you.

CLAIRE: You couldn't stay out of the water. You're like a fish when you get near water.

GERRY: I hate it.

CLAIRE: You taught me everything I know.

GERRY: I never taught you.

CLAIRE: You taught me how to crawl.

GERRY: Someone else must have.

CLAIRE: It took you hours to teach me but you did it. The first part was the easiest. That was teaching me how to stroke. I can see us now, standing in water up to our knees and you forcing me to bend over and stroke with my arms. I wasn't very good at first but I picked it up fast.

> *Claire bends over. She brings her right arm up and forward in a circular motion. Gerry drinks some more beer as he watches her.*

Right.

> *She brings her left arm up and over in a stroke.*

Left.

> *She repeats her strokes.*

Right. Left. Right. Left. Right. Left. Right. Left.

> *She stops and straightens up.*

Then came the hard part. That was learning how to breathe properly. That took a long time, didn't it?

GERRY: I never taught you how to breathe.

CLAIRE: Of course you did.

> *Claire bends over again. She strokes with her arms.*

Right. Left. Right. Left.

> *She shows him how she learned to breathe. She turns her head to her right as she strokes with her left arm.*

In.

> *She turns her head back as she strokes with her right arm. Then she strokes with her left arm, turning her head again.*

Out.

> *Claire repeats the same process.*

In.

> *She repeats it.*

Out.

> *She repeats it.*

In.

> *She repeats it.*

Out.

> *She stops and straightens up.*

It didn't take me long to pick it up. One day I was a beginner and the next I felt as if I had been doing it all my life. It was really something when I could swim out beside you to the raft and you didn't have to help me.

GERRY: I already told you before. I never swam with you to any raft.

CLAIRE: Sure you did. You used to spend every afternoon on the raft, soaking up the sun. And whenever it got too hot for you, you'd dive into the water, swim around and then come back to the raft.

GERRY: I don't like to suntan.

CLAIRE: Those two girls sure liked to.

GERRY: What two girls?

CLAIRE: Those two girls who spent the afternoon with you on the raft. They liked the way you moved through the water. They liked the way you stroked with your arms, the way you moved your legs, the way you turned your head to breathe in and out. They liked everything about you. They wanted you. You know how to turn on a chick. They couldn't wait for you to do it. You could have laid them right there on the raft if you wanted.

GERRY: Is that right?

CLAIRE: It was obvious enough. All the suggestive movements they were making.

GERRY: Such as?

CLAIRE: Such as running their hands up and down their bodies.

GERRY: I didn't notice anything.

CLAIRE: That's impossible.

GERRY: Not if I wasn't there.

CLAIRE: You were there. You were lying between the two of them. You were talking and having a good time. I still don't see how you couldn't have laid them.

GERRY: Maybe I did.

CLAIRE: What did you say?

GERRY: I said maybe I did lay them.

CLAIRE: And when did you do that? I was watching you all the time.

GERRY: I guess you must have missed something then.

CLAIRE: You never told me about this before.

GERRY: You never brought it up.

CLAIRE: How was it?

GERRY: It was all right.

> *Gerry turns off the tape recorder.*

CLAIRE: Since when has that been on?

GERRY: Since I turned it on.

> *Gerry reverses the tape on the tape recorder. Claire walks up to him.*

CLAIRE: You never told me you were recording. You bastard. You said you'd tell me when you were taping. You said there would be no more of it. You know how much I hate it. You can play back what I said whenever you feel like it. You can edit it, mix it, transform it, fuck with it any way you want to. You do that all the time. You twist things and make them unnatural. You change everything I say. You have to change everything into what you believe is the truth.

Gerry doesn't pay any attention to her. He's heard it a thousand times before. He puts the tape on play but it's not the right place. He reverses the tape again and then stops it, tries it on play and then turns it off.

GERRY: I want you to listen to this.

CLAIRE: Well, maybe I don't want to.

He puts the tape on play. Claire puts her index fingers against her ears when she hears herself talking on the tape.

(on tape) I didn't help him. He undressed on one side of the bed while I undressed on the other. He hung his shirt on a hanger and even folded his pants properly, and hung them up too. I guess he doesn't like them getting creased. *(pause)* So there we were, looking at each other across the bed. We climbed in between the sheets and he put his arms around me and I put my arms around him. He kissed me on the lips and I kissed him back. Shall I go on?

Pause in the tape. Claire sits on the sofa.

Do you want me to go on? I can if you want. I don't mind if you want to hear all about it.

Pause. Gerry turns off the tape recorder. Claire is still holding her fingers against her ears. Gerry lights a cigarette. Finally Claire takes her fingers from her ears.

(herself) I never said that. *(pause)* I never said anything like that in my life.

GERRY: You said it a few minutes ago.

CLAIRE: Like hell I did!

GERRY: I was in this room when you said it.

CLAIRE: Like hell you were.

GERRY: I heard you with my own two ears.

CLAIRE: Then you need a hearing aid.

GERRY: You refuse to believe it.

CLAIRE: You twist everything.

GERRY: You refuse to believe in your own voice.

CLAIRE: You reduce it to what you want. That isn't me anymore.

GERRY: It sounds like it to me.

CLAIRE: It doesn't to me.

GERRY: This machine doesn't ever lie.

CLAIRE: Screw the machine!

GERRY: It's objective. It doesn't have a grudge against anyone. It doesn't have any hang-ups. All you do is feed it electricity and tapes. If anything makes a sound, this will get it. If there's a voice somewhere, this will record it. It will record all the fears, all the laughter, all the dreams. All the variations of existence. It eliminates the physicality of people. The sweating armpits, the smelly feet, the bulging stomachs, the sagging breasts, the thinning hair. Only their voices are left. Only their sounds remain.

> *Claire approaches Gerry as he talks. She stands behind him, holding her beer bottle over his head. She pours a little beer on his head. Gerry doesn't move.*

CLAIRE: Maybe you'd better turn your machine on, Gerry. Maybe you should be getting all this down. Something's dripping on you.

> *She pours some more beer on his head but he still doesn't move. She's finding it hard not to laugh.*

I know what I'll do. I'll baptize you. I'll baptize you in the name of the machine.

> *She stands beside Gerry now.*

Are you ready?

> *She pours more beer on his head.*

(solemnly) I baptize you, Gerry, in the name of the daddy machine and the mommy machine and all the brother and sister machines . . .

> *She's laughing now. Gerry brushes off some drops of beer which fell on the tape recorder.*

Awwwwwwwwww! It got wet! It got wet from the beer! Poor little machine. Maybe it drowned in all that beer. Maybe it got all fucked up. You feeling fucked up, machine? Some of those dials going around the wrong way? That's too bad. You were such a nice little machine. Such an efficient one. It's hard finding ones like you these days. Machines just aren't what they used to be. Because you know what?

> *She bends down, close to the tape recorder.*

(she whispers) Because they make machines which break down quickly these days. They get neurotic and then they get psychotic and then they *(loud)* FREAK RIGHT OUT! That's right. That's what happens these days. *(she pauses)* Maybe you'd like some more beer. Maybe you're really thirsty. How about it? Would you like some more?

> *Claire walks into the kitchen, taking her empty bottle with her. She opens the fridge, takes out two bottles and opens them.*
>
> *Gerry pulls up his shirt and with the bottom of it he wipes off the tape recorder. She comes back in with a beer in each hand and sees him drying off the tape recorder. Gerry blocks her way to the table.*

What's the matter?

> *Gerry puts his right hand against her cheek and caresses it as he talks.*

GERRY: You shouldn't have done that. The machine doesn't like to get wet.

CLAIRE: You don't scare me.

GERRY: I'm not trying to scare you. I'm trying to talk some sense into you.

CLAIRE: I know what I'm doing.

GERRY: You have to respect other people's property.

CLAIRE: You have to respect people's privacy.

GERRY: You can't go around wrecking things.

CLAIRE: I spilled a little beer, that's all.

GERRY: One day you might pour out a whole bottle.

Gerry takes the two bottles of beer out of her hands and puts them on the table. Claire tries to move away from him but he grabs her arm.

GERRY: I know this man and woman. One day she did something he didn't like and he got very angry.

CLAIRE: Is that right?

GERRY: That's right, baby. He was pissed off about it. He started to mouth off to her but that didn't do him any good because she mouthed back.

CLAIRE: My heart bleeds.

GERRY: He starts slapping her around. On the head, in the mouth. She doesn't like that very much.

CLAIRE: I don't think she would.

Gerry pulls Claire onto the sofa and sits astride her chest as he talks. She fights back and flails at him with her hands, but he grabs them and forces them down.

GERRY: He starts punching her. In the stomach. At her breasts. She starts to cry. She tries to run away. He keeps punching her. Slapping her. She falls down, begs him to stop. He kicks her in the side. She falls over. He kicks her in the face. Her nose starts to bleed. She puts her hands over her face to protect herself. He kicks her in the back. He laughs at this point. He laughs a long time as she lies on the floor.

Pause. Gerry's sneer breaks into a laugh. He takes out a cigarette, lights it and holds it an inch above her skin in various places as he talks.

Then he unzips her dress and forces her out of it. He lights a cigarette. He puts the burning cigarette against her shoulder. She screams and jumps away. He kicks her in the side and she lies still. He kneels down and burns her stomach and her breasts. She doesn't say anything. She only rocks her head back and forth slowly. He watches her to see how long she can stand it. He waits for her to open her bloody mouth and ask him to stop. He waits for her to say the one word which will make him stop.

Gerry has her cheeks pinched between his fingers.

CLAIRE: You're hurting me.

GERRY: I am?

CLAIRE: Yes, you are.

GERRY: *(he squeezes harder)* I'm sorry.

CLAIRE: Stop it.

GERRY: Stop what?

CLAIRE: Stop it please.

GERRY: All right.

> *Gerry relaxes his grip.*

CLAIRE: You can let go now.

> *Pause. Gerry lets go. He gets off her and sits at the end of the sofa. Claire raises her knees and sits up slowly at the other end. Then she stands, walks to the table and has a drink from her beer. She lights a cigarette and walks back to the sofa. Gerry gets off the sofa, kneels in front of her, lifts up her dress and dries his head with it. When he's finished, he looks up at her.*

Thanks.

GERRY: You're welcome.

CLAIRE: You never told me what happened to the woman.

GERRY: What do you mean?

CLAIRE: Did she give in? Did he force her to talk?

GERRY: I don't think so.

CLAIRE: That must have made him feel terrible.

GERRY: It made him feel quite proud. She had a lot of guts to take pain like that. She's a special kind of woman.

> *Pause. Claire sits on the sofa. Gerry leans against it, watching her.*

You know what happened afterwards.

CLAIRE: Yes, I do.

GERRY: He knelt over her and kissed the burns on her body.

CLAIRE: But she didn't move for a long time.

GERRY: Not for a very long time.

CLAIRE: Finally she began to respond.

GERRY: She began kissing him.

CLAIRE: Running her fingers through his hair.

GERRY: Kissing him on the neck.

CLAIRE: Stroking his chest.

GERRY: Kissing him on the shoulders.

CLAIRE: Touching his arms.

GERRY: Kissing his hands.

CLAIRE: Stroking his thighs.

GERRY: Kissing.

CLAIRE: Bleeding.

GERRY: She was still bleeding from her mouth.

CLAIRE: So she took some of the blood

GERRY: And smeared it over his cheeks.

CLAIRE: She took some more of it

GERRY: And spread it on his forehead.

CLAIRE: She took some more

GERRY: And rubbed it all over his chest.

CLAIRE: Around his nipples.

GERRY: Around his navel.

CLAIRE: She kept rubbing it into his body.

GERRY: Then he took some blood

CLAIRE: And put it on her shoulders.

GERRY: He took some more

CLAIRE: And spread it on her burns.

GERRY: He took more

CLAIRE: And rubbed it all over her belly.

GERRY: They lay there together

CLAIRE: Side by side

GERRY: Looking into each other's eyes.

CLAIRE: The wet blood glistening

GERRY: On their bodies.

CLAIRE: Waiting.

GERRY: Watching.

CLAIRE: Waiting for the other to make

GERRY: The first move.

Pause. They watch each other.

CLAIRE: You can tell me.

Pause. Neither of them move.

GERRY: Come on.

CLAIRE: I want to hear what you have to say.

Pause.

GERRY: You'll have to get closer than that.

CLAIRE: If you want to whisper in my ear.

Pause. Gerry stands and goes to the table. He takes the cassette out of the recorder.

What are you doing?

GERRY: There's something I want you to hear.

CLAIRE: Maybe I want to hear what you have to say.

GERRY: What's that, Claire?

CLAIRE: I'd rather listen to you for a change.

> *Gerry takes a cassette out of his pocket and puts it in the tape recorder.*

You know. I had forgotten all about that man and woman.

GERRY: You had?

CLAIRE: We haven't seen them for a long time. I wonder how they're doing.

GERRY: Probably as well as can be expected these days.

CLAIRE: I wonder if they still get along with each other. What do you think?

> *Gerry turns the recorder on to play. At first you hear nothing, then you hear a subway train coming out of a tunnel and into a station. It runs along the platform and then stops, its brakes screeching. Doors open. People come out, pushing and shoving, muttering, talking. People get on the train. The doors close. The train moves out of the station. Al begins to talk.*

AL: *(on tape)* Most people don't like to think about what's real or not. Take where we are right now. Most people would say we're riding on a subway and leave it at that. But what's behind the walls of this tunnel? Tons of rock and dirt. And what's it doing? It's pressing in on these walls from every direction. All that dirt and rock is pressing in twenty-four hours a day, looking for faults, looking for cracks in the tunnel. And when it finds one, it will build up the pressure. It might take a couple days or a week. Perhaps a year. But that pressure will become more and more intense, until eventually that crack has to widen and let all that dirt and rock through.

> *Pause as Al pauses in the tape. Claire stands and walks to the table. Gerry sits in the chair.*

(on tape) I can remember when I was walking once. A woman was at the other end of the street when suddenly the sidewalk in front of her collapsed and sank ten feet. She stopped. She was in a state of shock. She knew she could have been on that section of the sidewalk. She was shocked because she'd expected it to remain stable. She'd forgotten that there was as much going on underneath the ground as there was above it. The trouble was she had certain expectations. That's something you do when you live in the future. I don't do that. I don't believe in anything anymore. I expect everything to be false.

> *Claire turns off the tape recorder.*

GERRY: What did you do that for?

CLAIRE: That's enough.

GERRY: He wasn't finished yet.

CLAIRE: It was enough for me.

GERRY: What's wrong?

CLAIRE: There's nothing wrong.

GERRY: There must be something. It didn't bother me.

CLAIRE: There's something abnormal about it all.

GERRY: I don't see anything wrong.

CLAIRE: Well. Then there's something abnormal about him.

GERRY: About him?

CLAIRE: That's right.

GERRY: He's as ordinary as you or me.

CLAIRE: Then we must be abnormal too, listening to him.

GERRY: You must be joking.

CLAIRE: I wish I was.

> *Gerry pushes down the play button on the tape recorder.*

AL: *(on tape)* I expect everyone to be hiding something. I expect everyone to lie. You have to protect yourself these days. There's no question —

> *Claire turns off the tape recorder.*

GERRY: You really mean it, don't you?

> *She takes the cassette out of the recorder.*

What are you doing?

> *She picks up Gerry's lighter off the table, flicks it, producing the flame. She slowly brings the flame closer to the cassette, until it is underneath it. She smiles as she does it. Gerry stands.*

Claire. You can't do that. That's a good tape. That has a good recording on it.

> *Gerry moves around the table after her. She moves away from him, still holding the flame under the cassette.*

What are you doing? You must be crazy.

CLAIRE: I'm not the one who's crazy around here.

GERRY: Give it to me.

> *Claire laughs. They move around the table slowly, Gerry chasing. Claire backing away.*

Give me that tape.

CLAIRE: You'll have to catch me first.

GERRY: That isn't yours to fool around with.

CLAIRE: It is if I have it in my hands.

> *Gerry lunges for it but misses. She tries to burn him with the lighter but misses too.*

GERRY: You bitch! You tried to burn me.

CLAIRE: Careful, Gerry. You might get scorched.

They stop on opposite sides of the table.

GERRY: You know I'll catch you eventually.

CLAIRE: That's what you say.

GERRY: What are you waiting for?

CLAIRE: For you.

GERRY: Why don't you give it to me?

CLAIRE: So you can play it again?

GERRY: I won't play it again.

CLAIRE: That's easy enough to say.

GERRY: I promise I won't.

CLAIRE: You always were good at making promises.

GERRY: What do you want me to do?

CLAIRE: How am I supposed to know?

They move around the table again.

GERRY: Please, Claire. Give it back to me.

CLAIRE: What did you say?

GERRY: I said please give it back.

CLAIRE: I never thought you'd do it.

GERRY: Do what?

CLAIRE: Say please.

They stop on opposite sides of the table again.

GERRY: Well. It wasn't that hard to say.

> *She offers him the cassette. He leans over the table, takes hold of it and then she quickly passes the flame under his hand. He pulls back his hand. She laughs.*

Goddamn it! That hurt!

CLAIRE: It was supposed to.

GERRY: What did you do that for?

CLAIRE: Because I felt like burning you.

GERRY: I ought to punch you in the face.

CLAIRE: Go ahead, if you feel like it.

GERRY: I really ought to.

> *Pause. Claire puts the lighter down and moves around the table to Gerry. She takes hold of his hand.*

CLAIRE: Let me look.

GERRY: What for? So you can burn it again?

CLAIRE: This will make it better.

Claire kisses his hand.

How's that?

GERRY: It's feeling better already.

> *Claire picks up her beer and takes a long drink from it as she leans against the table. Gerry examines the cassette for damage.*

CLAIRE: There's nothing wrong with it.

GERRY: How do you know?

CLAIRE: Because I never brought it close enough, that's why.

GERRY: You're lucky you didn't.

CLAIRE: I never would have.

GERRY: Is that right?

> *Pause. She smiles and takes another drink.*

So you had it all planned from the start?

> *Pause. Gerry re-examines the cassette. Claire takes a dog whistle from under her dress, puts it to her lips and blows on it. There is no audible sound. She blows on it again.*

What are you trying to do exactly?

CLAIRE: I'm playing something for you.

GERRY: It won't do you much good. That's a dog whistle.

CLAIRE: That's your problem, isn't it?

GERRY: What do you mean by that?

> *Pause. She blows on the whistle again.*

CLAIRE: I played a little number with this today.

GERRY: You did?

CLAIRE: A little tune.

GERRY: Is that so?

CLAIRE: I found this in the park near the bridge today. I bet you didn't know that from the park you can see the small platform under the bridge.

GERRY: I didn't even know there was a platform.

> *Gerry takes a long hit off his beer.*

CLAIRE: Well, there is. And on this platform under the concrete supports, people do whatever they want because they think they're out of sight. They think they're concealed from the world. Winos drink their wine and sleep it off there. Kids sniff glue and smoke grass here. *(she pauses)* Do you want me to go on? I can stop if you want me to.

GERRY: Don't stop now. You're getting more boring every minute.

CLAIRE: However, there weren't any kids under the bridge. But there were two men. One young and one about your age, Gerry. In fact, he seemed very familiar. Maybe he was a friend. Do any of your friends hang around down by the bridge?

GERRY: Not that I know of.

CLAIRE: You sure?

GERRY: I don't know everything they do. I'm not a cop.

Pause. Gerry sits on the sofa. Claire stands by the table.

Well. How about it?

CLAIRE: How about what?

GERRY: Aren't you going to tell me what the two men were doing?

CLAIRE: I thought you didn't want me to go on. I thought I was boring you.

GERRY: You weren't boring me. I don't know what made me say that.

CLAIRE: It was your fine sense of humour.

GERRY: Yeah. I guess that's what it was.

Pause. Claire has a drink from her beer.

CLAIRE: The two men stood up against the wall. The young one had his pants rolled down to his knees. The older man was going at him.

GERRY: Going at him?

CLAIRE: You know. Homo-sexually.

GERRY: Is that right?

CLAIRE: That's right.

GERRY: I thought it didn't bother you.

CLAIRE: It doesn't. It's just that these men seemed familiar.

GERRY: Was it crowded in the park?

CLAIRE: Not really.

GERRY: Do you think anyone else saw these men?

CLAIRE: I don't know. They might have.

GERRY: Did you see anyone around?

CLAIRE: Not where I was.

GERRY: How long did you watch them?

CLAIRE: Long enough.

GERRY: And how long was that?

CLAIRE: You know. You certainly ask a lot of questions for someone who wasn't interested.

GERRY: I never said I wasn't interested.

CLAIRE: I thought you did.

GERRY: Well, you must have made a mistake.

CLAIRE: I guess so.

>*Pause. Claire yawns.*

GERRY: Tired?

CLAIRE: I think I'll go to bed soon.

GERRY: Now about these men.

CLAIRE: What about them?

GERRY: What exactly did you see?

CLAIRE: I saw what they were doing.

GERRY: Did you see their faces?

CLAIRE: *(yawning again)* Not exactly.

GERRY: What do you mean not exactly?

CLAIRE: Well, I saw enough of their faces.

GERRY: Enough?

CLAIRE: To tell that one was older and one was younger.

GERRY: And that's all?

CLAIRE: *(yawning again)* Yeah, I'm afraid so. Their faces were in the shadows most of the time.

>*Claire heads for the doorway but Gerry gets up and stands in the doorway, blocking her way.*

GERRY: Where are you going?

CLAIRE: To sleep.

GERRY: You can't go yet. You haven't told me why these men seemed so familiar.

CLAIRE: I don't know. They just seemed to be.

GERRY: How did they seem to be?

CLAIRE: Well, the way they stood. The way they moved around. It all seemed very familiar to me.

GERRY: Is that it?

CLAIRE: You're worried, aren't you?

GERRY: What do I have to be worried about?

CLAIRE: I don't know. You're the one who's asking all the questions.

GERRY: I wanted to find out why you thought these two men seemed so familiar. That's all. That's no crime.

CLAIRE: No, it isn't.

>*Gerry leans against the wall.*

GERRY: I thought you were going to sleep.

CLAIRE: I was until you stopped me.

GERRY: Sorry. I didn't mean to . . .

CLAIRE: You coming?

GERRY: I'll be right in but I have to set the alarm.

> *Gerry moves to the table.*

CLAIRE: All right. You know what?

GERRY: What?

CLAIRE: They kissed each other.

GERRY: Who did?

CLAIRE: Those two men. They kissed each other on the mouth for a long time.
What do you think of that?

GERRY: I don't know.

CLAIRE: Isn't that something?

> *Claire walks up the hall into the bedroom. Gerry looks for the
> second alarm clock, which he finds under a magazine in front of
> the sofa. He winds it up, resets the time and the alarm on it.
> Then he turns off the lamp and blocks of light spill into the living
> room from the kitchen and hall. He puts the cassette Claire tried
> to burn in the tape recorder. He reverses the tape and then stops
> it. He starts the tape and as it runs he stands with his hands rest-
> ing on the table.*

AL: *(on tape)* That's something you do when you believe in the future. I don't do
that. I don't believe in anything anymore. I expect everything to be false. I
expect everyone to be hiding something. I expect everyone to lie. You have
to protect yourself these days. There's no question about that. I don't believe in my past. I know what happened to me yesterday and the day before
that and even a year ago. But I don't know if it really happened or if I just
thought it did. I can't trust my imagination anymore. It constructs places I
haven't been; it makes up conversations with people I haven't had. What
happened to me an hour ago could be true and it could be false. I'm not honest
with my past. No one is honest with his past. It's just like history in books.
It's constructed as it should have been, not as it really was. Because it's
always written after it happens. The language doesn't help either. Words
mean so many things to so many people. I can't believe in what I say or other
people say. I expect them to misunderstand me. *(Al pauses)* I do believe in
what I'm doing now. I am speaking into this microphone and I know my
words are being recorded on magnetic tape. That's all I know. This is all I
can believe in. My voice. My words. My hand holding the microphone. My
sweating palm.

> *The tape keeps running. We hear the sound of the subway train
> as it runs along the tracks in the tunnel. Gerry stands still for a
> long time and then he punches the stop button. He picks up his
> alarm clock and turns out the kitchen light. He stands in the
> kitchen doorway and looks at the tape recorder, almost as if he
> hoped it could speak, then he crosses the room, walks up the hall
> to the bedroom. The hall light goes out and the living room is
> dark. Silence except for the ticking alarm clock on the table.*

Act Three

Darkness. Al sits at the table. He plays a few notes on the trumpet and then stops. He waits. Then he plays a few more notes on it. He stops and waits again.

Gerry comes out of the bedroom and turns on the hall light, which spills into the living room. Al holds his hand to his eyes. The alarm clock reads two o'clock in the morning. Al gets up and sits in the easy chair, which is in relative darkness. Gerry comes down the hall and stands in the doorway. He looks like he's been sleeping.

GERRY: What are you doing?

AL: I'm sitting.

GERRY: You don't have to sit in the dark.

AL: I like it.

GERRY: How could you possibly like it?

AL: I don't know. I just do.

        Pause.

GERRY: What's all the racket about?

AL: What racket?

GERRY: The noise you were making.

AL: That wasn't noise. That was my trumpet. I was playing it.

GERRY: So that's what you were doing.

AL: That's right.

        Pause.

GERRY: Where's Claire?

AL: Isn't she with you?

GERRY: No, she isn't.

AL: Oh, I thought she was with you.

GERRY: Did she talk with you?

AL: About what?

GERRY: I don't know. She said she wanted to have a talk with you.

AL: Well, she did that all right.

GERRY: How did it go?

        Pause. Al shrugs his shoulders. Gerry stands beside the easy chair.

  I hope you know that you don't have to wait.

AL: I know that.

GERRY: You can go if you want. No one's forcing you to stay here.

AL: I know that too.

GERRY: Good. As long as it's clear why you're here. I wouldn't want there to be any misunderstanding.

AL: Why should there be one?

GERRY: I don't know. I thought we should bring things . . .

AL: What do you think I am?

GERRY: . . . out in the open.

AL: A moron or something? Is that what you think?

GERRY: I didn't say you were a moron.

AL: You might not have said it but that's what you meant.

GERRY: What I meant?

AL: I can tell what you're really saying, you know. I'm not the moron you think I am. I know how people say one thing and mean something completely different. I get the message, Gerry. You don't have to pound it into my head.

GERRY: Pound what into your head?

AL: Don't play innocent with me.

GERRY: I'm not playing anything with you. I wish you'd say what's on your mind.

AL: If I said what was on my mind. If I said ten per cent of what was on my mind, they'd take me outside and shoot me. The world isn't ready for people that think like me. Most people go around without even knowing what's in their mind, let alone saying it.

> *Pause. Gerry turns on the lamp.*

I don't see why you had to turn it on.

> *Pause. Gerry directs the beam of light from the lamp at Al.*

What are you looking at?

GERRY: At you.

AL: What's so special about me?

GERRY: I'm waiting for you to tell me what's on your mind.

AL: You don't want to hear what I have to say.

> *Gerry puts the lamp back in its original position.*

GERRY: I certainly do, Al.

AL: Don't bullshit me.

GERRY: You know, you don't have to be afraid of telling me.

AL: I'm not afraid.

GERRY: Then what's stopping you?

AL: You wouldn't understand.

GERRY: And how do you know that?

AL: I can tell.

GERRY: I'm glad you can because I certainly can't.

> *Pause.*

This waiting really seems to be bothering you.

> *Pause.*

It used to bother me but I managed to learn to live with it. You'll learn to get used to it. Once you do that, everything will be better. You'll have a brighter outlook on things.

> *Pause. Al shakes his head slowly.*

You really don't like to be kept waiting, do you?

> *Pause. Gerry sits at the table.*

You don't think it's right, do you? You don't think you deserve to be treated like this.

> *Pause.*

Do you think you're anything special? Anything significant?

AL: Why all the questions?

GERRY: Why not?

AL: You a cop or something?

GERRY: Do you want me to be one?

AL: What's that supposed to mean?

GERRY: I can be one if you want. I can ask you a lot of questions.

AL: You already seem to be doing that.

GERRY: But you're not answering them, Al.

AL: No one said I had to.

GERRY: *(he whispers)* I can interrogate you if you want.

AL: I don't need to be interrogated.

> *Pause. Al stands and moves to the hall doorway.*

GERRY: I can pretend to be the cop and you can pretend to be the criminal.

> *Al stops in the doorway. He doesn't turn around. Gerry watches him.*

I can ask you personal questions. Embarrassing ones. I can make you talk. I can make you tell me what I want to know.

> *Al turns and faces him.*

AL: *(daring him)* Is that right?

GERRY: Are you interested?

AL: I'm thirsty. I need a beer.

> *Al walks past him and goes into the kitchen. Al opens the fridge,*

gets out a beer and opens it. Gerry puts a cassette in the tape re-
corder and puts it on record.

Al leans in the kitchen doorway with his beer. Gerry lights a
cigarette and then walks up to Al.

GERRY: You see this cigarette?

AL: Yeah.

GERRY: You know, if I move it closer, it will eventually touch your chest.

AL: I guess it would.

GERRY: And when it touches your chest, it will burn it. And it will keep burning until I take it away.

> *Gerry unbuttons the top three buttons of Al's shirt and puts the*
> *cigarette close to his chest. Al doesn't move.*

I guess that would leave quite a scar.

AL: It sure would.

GERRY: Do you like scars?

AL: Not really.

GERRY: Does that mean yes or no?

AL: It means I don't worry about them.

GERRY: Most people worry. They don't like having scars. They don't like
having anything to do with them.

AL: I guess I'm not like most people then.

GERRY: I guess you aren't.

> *Pause. Gerry pulls Al's shirt open and flicks cigarette ash in-*
> *side it. Al doesn't move. Then Gerry walks away, stopping on*
> *the other side of the table.*

You're not normal, are you?

AL: I suppose I am.

GERRY: You suppose you are?

AL: I think I am.

GERRY: You think you are? You mean you don't know?

AL: Of course I know.

GERRY: Well, are you or aren't you?

AL: I suppose I'm like everyone else. I have a head. I have hair on my head.
I have two ears to hear things with. I have a face. I have two eyes which see.
A nose which smells. A mouth which eats and drinks. And inside my mouth
I have teeth.

> *Pause. He opens his mouth and shows Gerry his teeth clenched*
> *together.*

I also have a tongue which is what I talk with.

> *Pause. He sticks out his tongue at Gerry. As he talks, he moves slowly towards Gerry until he stands in front of him.*

I have a neck. I have shoulders. I have two arms, my right and left arm. At the ends of my arms I have hands. Each hand has four fingers and a thumb. I have two armpits, which sweat and smell. I have a chest and stomach. Below my stomach are my balls and my prick. I piss with my prick. Sometimes it becomes erect. Sometimes it becomes wet and sticky with sperm. My sperm. Like minute fish swimming wherever the current takes them.

> *Pause. Al puts his foot on the chair and his knee up against Gerry's chest.*

I have two legs, a right and left leg. At the bottom of my legs, I have feet. Each foot has four small toes and one big toe. I walk like everyone else. I put one foot forward and then the next foot forward. One foot at a time until I get where I want to go. That's how everyone else does it.

> *Pause. Neither of them moves. Then Al lifts his foot off the chair and stands back from Gerry.*

GERRY: Where were you last night?

AL: In my apartment.

GERRY: Did you go out at all?

AL: I went out once.

GERRY: Where?

AL: I went for a ride on the subway.

GERRY: Where?

AL: To the end of the line.

GERRY: Who were you going to see?

AL: No one.

GERRY: Didn't you see a woman?

AL: No.

GERRY: You sure about that?

AL: I'm positive.

> *Pause. Al takes a drink of his beer. Gerry picks up the alarm clock on the table and winds it up.*

GERRY: I think you're lying. That's what I think you're doing.

AL: I told you what happened.

GERRY: How come it contradicts with what I know?

AL: I don't know. I went for a ride on the subway. And as far as I know, it isn't a crime if you pay your fare. You can ride to the end of the line and ride back to the other end of the line. You can do that all night if you want. It's up to you what you do with your free time. That's the basis of this country. At least that's what they tell me.

Gerry stands and walks to Al. He still has the clock in his hand.

GERRY: You see this?

AL: Yeah.

GERRY: You hear it?

AL: Yeah.

Gerry puts the clock against Al's ear.

GERRY: You can hear every tick now.

Pause. Gerry holds the clock against Al's ear.

You know. You can't afford to lie to me.

AL: I haven't lied to you.

GERRY: I'm afraid you have. You told me you rode to the end of the line. You told me you didn't see anyone last night.

AL: And I didn't.

GERRY: You don't have much time left, you know. All those seconds and minutes. They vanish pretty fast. All those hours and days. They're gone sooner than you think.

AL: I don't think I understand —

GERRY: You understand all right. Time is a very necessary process because it's how we compare ourselves. It's how we evaluate ourselves. Without our time zones we would be lost.

AL: I don't see what this has got to do with —

Gerry takes the clock away.

GERRY: You know what this is all about. I want the truth and here you are, telling me these phony stories, when you could be saving your time —

AL: You're the one who's wasting —

GERRY: I'm trying to save it for you. Remember that.

Pause. Gerry sets the alarm on the clock and puts it on the table.

GERRY: So where did you go last night?

AL: I already told you. I went for a ride underground.

GERRY: And you didn't meet anyone?

AL: That's right.

GERRY: Did you meet someone on the subway?

AL: No.

GERRY: You didn't have a rendezvous?

AL: No, I didn't.

GERRY: What was her name?

AL: I don't know what you're talking about.

GERRY: What was she like?

AL: I still don't know . . .

GERRY: Was she old? Or was she young?

AL: I've nothing to tell you.

GERRY: Was she good looking? Or was she ugly?

>*Pause.*

Was she what you wanted in a woman?

>*Pause.*

Did she allow you to touch her?

>*Pause.*

Did she let you kiss her?

>*Pause.*

Did she make love with you?

>*Pause.*

Did she want to?

>*Pause. Gerry approaches Al.*

Maybe she didn't want to. Maybe she didn't want you around anymore. Maybe she told you that and you wouldn't believe her. Maybe she said she couldn't afford any more time with you.

AL: That's not true!

GERRY: What isn't?

AL: *(too quickly)* I don't know what you're talking about.

GERRY: What isn't true, Al? Come on. You can tell me all about it.

>*Pause. Gerry is face to face with Al. Then he leans next to his mouth, so Al can whisper into his ear.*

No one else has to hear, you know.

>*Pause. Al doesn't move or say anything. Gerry straightens up.*

All right then. You got on the subway and rode to the end of the line. Then what happened?

AL: I rode back and got off at my stop.

GERRY: Did you notice anything?

AL: No.

GERRY: Did you notice any people?

AL: No.

GERRY: Are you sure a couple didn't get on?

AL: Positive.

GERRY: Let's say a couple did get on. Let's say the woman gave you a special kind of look, which meant she wanted you to follow them.

AL: No couple got on.

GERRY: Did you follow them?

AL: I rode back to my station.

GERRY: So you didn't follow them home to see where they lived?

AL: I'd never do a thing like that.

GERRY: This is a free country. You can follow people if you want to. You can move around wherever you like.

AL: Some people can.

GERRY: Let's say you did follow them home last night. Let's say you waited until the man was out and then you visited the woman.

AL: I'd never do anything like that.

GERRY: You wouldn't even consider it?

> *Gerry goes and sits on the table. He watches Al, who moves around the room near the walls.*

AL: Never.

GERRY: Not the slightest possibility?

AL: Nope.

GERRY: Why not?

AL: I don't go around doing things like that.

GERRY: Maybe the woman wanted to meet you.

AL: Maybe she did.

GERRY: Maybe the man wanted to meet you.

AL: Maybe he did.

GERRY: You never know until you try.

AL: No, I guess you don't.

GERRY: That couple could have changed the course of your life.

AL: I guess they could have.

GERRY: And you could have changed theirs.

AL: Maybe I already have.

GERRY: What do you mean?

AL: Maybe I already changed their lives.

GERRY: But you told me you didn't follow them home. That you wouldn't do anything like that.

AL: That's right. But maybe I talked to them on the subway.

GERRY: But you said no one got on.

AL: Let's say a couple did get on and I talked to them. Let's say I told them all I know about the underground.

GERRY: And how would that affect them?

AL: It could affect them in many ways. Couldn't it?

> *Al has stopped moving around the room.*

GERRY: Yes. I guess it could.

> *Gerry turns off the tape recorder, then puts it in reverse.*

AL: I didn't know that was on.

GERRY: I hope you don't mind.

AL: No, I don't mind.

> *Pause. Al comes up to him.*

You know things like that don't bother me at all.

GERRY: That's good.

> *Gerry stops the tape and puts it on play. But it isn't the right place, so he reverses it again, and then stops it.*

Because I want you to listen to this.

> *Al puts his hand on Gerry's hand and stops him from pushing the play button.*

AL: Maybe I don't want to.

GERRY: You are sore about me having it on.

AL: Maybe I am.

GERRY: I won't do it again.

AL: That's what you said last time.

GERRY: Let's not worry about it. I know you'll enjoy this.

AL: I'm glad you think so.

GERRY: I know Claire will love it.

AL: And how do you know that?

GERRY: She's loved everything you've done before.

AL: That doesn't mean she'll like this.

GERRY: She likes anything you do. You know that.

> *Al takes his hand away. Gerry pushes down the play button.*

AL: *(on tape)* I have two ears to hear things with. I have a face. I have two eyes which see. A nose which smells. A mouth which eats and drinks. And inside my mouth, I have teeth.

> *Pause in the tape. Al opens his mouth and shows Gerry his clenched teeth.*

I also have a tongue, which is what I talk with.

> *Pause in the tape. Al sticks out his tongue. He licks Gerry on the right cheek. Gerry sits still on the table.*

I have a neck. I have shoulders. I have two arms, my right and left arm. At the ends of my arms I have hands. Each hand has four fingers and a thumb.

> *Pause. Gerry turns off the tape recorder. Al licks Gerry on the left cheek with his tongue.*

GERRY: You've got me wet.

> *Pause.*

You've got both my cheeks wet.

> *Pause.*

What'd you do that for?

AL: Because I felt like it.

GERRY: Is that it?

> *Pause. Al goes and sits on the arm of the sofa.*

Is that the only reason? *(pause)* Is that all there is to it?

AL: What did you expect?

GERRY: Some kind of answer.

AL: *(he laughs)* As if you could be so lucky.

> *Pause. Al takes a drink from his beer.*

Well, Gerry.

GERRY: Well what?

AL: I don't think you told me where she went.

GERRY: She went out.

AL: I already know that. I asked you where she went.

GERRY: I don't know.

AL: No idea, eh?

GERRY: No idea at all.

> *Pause.*

AL: How long ago did she leave?

GERRY: I don't know exactly.

AL: But you usually know what time she leaves.

GERRY: I forgot to look.

AL: You forgot to look, did you?

GERRY: That's what happened.

AL: Did she leave half an hour ago?

GERRY: I think it was longer than that.

AL: An hour ago?

GERRY: I think it was somewhere around there.

AL: You think? You mean you don't know?

GERRY: I'm pretty sure it was then.

AL: So you're pretty sure now?

GERRY: That's right.

Pause.

AL: Was she walking?

GERRY: I imagine she was.

AL: You imagine? You mean you don't know?

GERRY: She probably is.

AL: She could be driving around, you know.

GERRY: Yes, she could.

AL: Or she could be parked at a drive-in, eating a hamburger. A lot of guys hang around drive-ins.

GERRY: I guess they do.

AL: She could even be in a bar, having a drink. You know what happens in bars, don't you?

GERRY: Nothing has to happen.

AL: She might be striking up a conversation with someone.

Pause. Gerry swings his legs back and forth under the table.

I said, she might be striking up a conversation with someone in the bar.

GERRY: I heard you.

AL: Do you think that's what she's doing?

GERRY: I don't know.

AL: You don't want to think about it, do you?

GERRY: I'm not worried about her. She can do what she wants. She can go where she wants. I can't tell her what to do.

Pause. Al drinks from his beer.

AL: What did she tell you then?

GERRY: Not much.

AL: I guess she couldn't have. You don't know much tonight, do you?

Pause. Al stands and approaches Gerry.

How are you and Claire getting along?

GERRY: We're getting along fine.

AL: No problems?

GERRY: None at all.

AL: No disagreements?

GERRY: Of course not.

AL: You sure about that?

GERRY: Positive.

AL: There must be something bothering you.

>*Gerry shakes his head.*

Some little thing.

>*Gerry shakes his head again.*

Something she said.

>*He shakes his head again. Al picks up the trumpet and offers it to him.*

GERRY: What are you giving me this for?

AL: To play on.

GERRY: I don't know how to play it.

AL: Then you should learn.

GERRY: But I'd sound awful.

AL: You just have to do something simple. Something easy.

GERRY: But I couldn't.

AL: Come on. You can play a little something for us. A little tune.

>*Gerry takes the toy trumpet.*

GERRY: I can't really.

AL: Everyone can play. Come on. Put it up to your lips.

>*Gerry raises the trumpet to his lips.*

That's it. Now pucker and blow into it.

>*Gerry blows into the trumpet but no sound comes out.*

You're not puckering right.

>*Gerry pushes down one key and produces a note.*

That's it. You've got the hang of it now.

>*Gerry presses down on the first key again, holding the note. Then he presses down on the second key, holding the note as long as the first one.*

Great. You're really going now.

>*Gerry presses down the first key, holds it. He presses down the second key, holds it. Then he presses down the third key and holds it as long as the first two.*

That's great!

>*Gerry gets off the table and walks around it, playing the trumpet. He presses the three keys in sequence. He repeats this simple tune as he walks.*

You're doing fine. Just fine.

Gerry goes past Al and around the table a second time. When he comes around to Al he stops in front of him.

What did you stop for? Keep going. Keep on going. You're doing just fine.

Gerry puts the end of the trumpet in Al's face and presses down on all the keys, producing one loud note. He keeps blowing until Al puts his hand up and covers the opening of the trumpet.

What did you do that for?

GERRY: Because I felt like it.

Pause. Al takes his hand from the trumpet.

I just remembered something. Claire left a message for you.

AL: She did?

GERRY: She gave it to me before she left.

AL: What's the message?

Gerry puts the trumpet on the table and takes a cassette tape out of his pocket. He holds it up and shakes it.

GERRY: It's in here.

AL: How come you didn't tell me about this before?

GERRY: I must have forgotten about it.

AL: I guess you must have.

GERRY: You want me to play it or not?

AL: Go right ahead.

Gerry takes a cassette out of the recorder and puts Claire's cassette in it. He turns it on to play. Claire is pacing in a room with a wooden floor as she talks.

CLAIRE: *(on tape)* I went out walking a couple of nights ago. It was quiet and the sky had clouded over, so there were no stars. I had just turned a corner when I heard this sound. I stopped and listened. It sounded like a man yelling for help, except it was as if he was trapped within a room. As if he was whispering. I tried to find where the sound was coming from but then it suddenly stopped. I soon discovered why. In the next block of the street a young man was lying with his legs down a manhole. The top half of his body was lying in the street. He had a plastic bag over his head with string tied around his neck. He had suffocated. I didn't know what to do. I couldn't tell whether he had tried to climb in the hole or out of it. I took hold of his hands and pulled him on to the street. I called for help. I must have called a hundred times but no one came. Then I went through his pockets. He didn't have any identification. No birth certificate. No social insurance card. No driver's licence. Nothing. Except for a book of poems by Mao Tse Tung.

Pause. Neither moves to shut off the tape.

GERRY: What'd she tell you something like that for?

AL: You figure it out. You're so smart.

GERRY: What's the matter?

AL: Nothing's the matter. Aren't you going to shut it off?

> *Pause. Gerry turns off the tape recorder.*

GERRY: The only reason I asked is because you looked like you were —

AL: Like I was what?

GERRY: Like you were.

AL: You don't have to lie to me, you know. You can tell me what's on your mind. I don't care what it is. I can take it.

GERRY: You looked shaken up after her message.

AL: How do you know how I should look?

GERRY: I didn't say I did. It just seemed that —

AL: How do you know what I feel? I don't know what you feel so how can you know about me? I may look terrible but I may feel great. The world would be a lot better off if people would leave other people alone and stop forcing them to act like they do.

GERRY: I wasn't forcing you. I noticed that what she said got you down.

AL: Maybe you thought it got me down. Maybe that's what you think a person should look like when he's down. But that doesn't mean I was.

> *Pause. Al sits on the arm of the sofa. Gerry suddenly goes to the framed photograph on the wall and takes it off its hook.*

GERRY: You know, I've always liked this one of you and me. I think it's the best of them all. What do you think? Do you think it's the best?

AL: We've never had our picture taken together.

GERRY: How can you say something like that?

> *Gerry shows Al the photograph.*

AL: That isn't me and you know it.

GERRY: *(he laughs)* That's not a very good joke.

AL: It wasn't supposed to be.

> *Gerry sits beside him on the sofa.*

GERRY: You know that we're going on a vacation soon.

AL: I didn't know that.

GERRY: But this time we'll have more fun. And we'll stay in a better motel. How would you like that? Would you like to stay at a better motel?

AL: I don't care what you do.

GERRY: You'll enjoy yourself even more this time. We'll sit in the bar and watch the couples dance. We'll just sit there and drink our drinks, and listen to the music and watch the people dance. It'll be relaxing, which is what a vacation is supposed to be.

AL: I never went to any motel with you.

GERRY: And if we don't like it inside the bar, we can always sit outside at a table. That's nice. Listening to the music in the dark, looking up at all the stars in the sky. I remember the last time we were so drunk that we started to count the stars.

AL: I never counted any.

GERRY: You kept counting even after I stopped. Except you complained how all the stars kept moving around and wouldn't stay still long enough to be counted.

Pause. Al stands and goes to the table.

You know, I can still remember all the hours we spent by the swimming pool.

AL: Maybe you can.

GERRY: That's where you taught me how to dive.

AL: I didn't teach you.

GERRY: You taught me how to dive off the high board.

AL: I don't know how to dive myself.

Al lights a cigarette.

GERRY: Of course you do. You're an excellent diver. I used to watch you for hours. You would run along the board and then take off in the air, your arms spread out in a perfect swan dive, your legs together, your point of entry into the water exactly where it should be. Everyone around the pool would stop and watch you. All their eyes were on you and your body. On your form. On your flight through the air.

AL: No one ever watched me dive.

Gerry stands, walks over to Al.

GERRY: And this time I'll try swimming in the deep end. I'll try to reach the bottom and stay down there, like you can. Maybe I'll get so good, that it will seem like second nature to me, like it is with you.

AL: It isn't second nature to me.

GERRY: What do you think? Will I be able to do it?

AL: How should I know?

GERRY: If I train long enough?

AL: I don't know.

GERRY: If I know how to hold my breath?

AL: I don't know.

GERRY: That's the secret, isn't it? You have to know how to control your breath when you're in the deep end. You'll teach me how to do that, won't you?

Pause. Al leaves Gerry and stands on the other side of the table.

You'll teach me breath control, won't you?

Pause.

You'll go with me on this vacation, won't you?

AL: Maybe.

GERRY: I know you'll enjoy yourself.

AL: I might.

GERRY: How about it? Are you coming?

AL: It sounds like a good idea. *(pause)* What about Claire?

GERRY: What about her?

AL: Is she coming?

GERRY: Do you want her to come?

AL: I do if she wants to.

GERRY: I don't think she will.

AL: How do you know that?

GERRY: I just do.

AL: Did you ask her already?

GERRY: No.

AL: Then how do you know?

> *Pause. Gerry hangs the photograph on the wall.*

I think she'll want to go.

GERRY: I doubt if she will.

AL: Why do you say that?

GERRY: She'd feel in the way.

AL: She wouldn't be in mine.

GERRY: I don't think she'd want to be around. Besides, she doesn't have the time right now.

AL: What do you mean?

GERRY: She can't afford the time.

AL: She doesn't have anything to do.

GERRY: You'd be surprised at what she has to do.

AL: Like what?

GERRY: You'd just be surprised at all the things she has to do.

> *Pause. Gerry walks back to the table.*

AL: I think I'll ask her why she can't come.

GERRY: You mean you're going to wait until she comes back?

AL: That's right.

GERRY: I think you'll have a long wait.

AL: What do you mean?

GERRY: It should be obvious by now, Al.

AL: What should?

GERRY: Why she isn't back yet. Why you've been waiting so long.

The alarm clock on the table rings.

AL: Aren't you going to shut it off?

GERRY: Why should I?

AL: I'm not going to.

GERRY: Neither am I.

> *Pause. Neither moves to turn off the clock. Finally it stops ringing.*

I'm afraid your time is up now.

AL: What are you talking about?

GERRY: It looks like you'll have to leave.

AL: You're kidding me.

GERRY: I wish I was, Al.

AL: You're joking.

GERRY: Not this time.

AL: You've never done this before. You've always let me stay if I wanted.

GERRY: I know.

AL: The subway isn't working now. How am I supposed to get to my place?

GERRY: You can always walk.

AL: I'm not leaving until she comes back.

GERRY: I wouldn't be too sure about that.

AL: Why not?

GERRY: You really mean to stay?

AL: That's right.

GERRY: Nothing would make you go?

AL: Unless you want to throw me out.

GERRY: I'm just making sure, that's all.

AL: Sure about what?

GERRY: I don't like rushing into these things.

AL: Into what things?

> *Pause. Gerry takes a plastic bag out of his pocket and holds it up.*

What's that for?

GERRY: You.

AL: For me?

GERRY: She wanted you to have it.

AL: You're kidding me.

GERRY: I wish I was.

AL: It seems pretty stupid to me. What am I supposed to do with that?

> *Pause.*

GERRY: She said you would know what it's for. She said you would know how to use it.

> *Pause. Al comes around the front of the table to Gerry.*

Is that true? Do you know how to use it?

> *Pause. Al takes the plastic bag from him.*

What are you going to do?

AL: What can I do? Just exactly what can I do?

GERRY: You don't have to do anything. You could leave.

AL: Yeah. I guess I could.

> *Pause. Al sits on the chair by the table. He looks at the plastic bag. Then he opens it and puts his hand inside it. Gerry watches him.*

But it wouldn't seem right. Not after everything that's happened.

GERRY: That still doesn't mean you have to do anything.

AL: I know that.

GERRY: You should think about it some more.

AL: I have thought about it. Ever since I can remember, I've been thinking about it. What I'm doing or where I am doesn't make any difference. Sleeping, eating, working, I think about it.

> *Al pauses. Gerry has already put a new cassette in the tape recorder. He puts it on record.*

The first time I talked to Claire I expected some kind of answer. Perhaps that was the problem. It isn't something you can look up in an encyclopaedia. I actually thought she could help me figure it all out. Where I was going and where I wanted to go. But she couldn't tell me the future. She couldn't even tell me what would happen an hour from now. No one can.

GERRY: You know. You'll feel different about this tomorrow.

AL: That's what I say to myself every day. That's what I said today. But it isn't any use. When tomorrow comes, I always feel the same.

> *Pause. Al takes his hand out of the bag.*

GERRY: Say. Do you remember the night we went drinking?

AL: Yeah. I remember it all right.

> *Al bends over and unties the knotted lace of his work boot. Then he undoes the lace from the boot.*

GERRY: We got drunk. We got really pissed. Remember how we were pouring beer over each other's head? Remember that? You said we were giving each other a shower.

AL: We got pretty crazy that night.

GERRY: I'll say we did. I don't think I've ever had a night like that one. We were so smashed we tried to fly. Remember that? You bet me that we could and I bet you that we couldn't. We got up on the wall and flapped our arms like crazy and then we jumped off. We were lucky we didn't break a leg.

AL: Yeah, we were.

Al takes the lace out of the boot.

GERRY: Then why don't we do that tomorrow? Why don't we go on one hell of a pub crawl? We haven't done something like that for a long time.

AL: I can't, Gerry.

GERRY: Sure you can.

AL: I've made up my mind.

GERRY: Really?

AL: Really.

GERRY: Nothing will change it?

AL: Not now.

Al lifts the plastic bag over his head.

GERRY: Wait a minute, Al.

Gerry picks up the microphone off the table and holds it in front of Al.

Will you say something? You can if you want. Just a few sentences. Or a few words. Or anything you feel like saying. It's customary to say a few last words. You know. How about it?

AL: I've got nothing to say anymore.

GERRY: You can't mean that.

AL: I can mean it all right.

Al lowers the plastic bag over his head.

GERRY: I know you won't mind me doing this, Al. I know that you understand why I have to do it. You understand, don't you? It's for Claire when she comes back. She'll like that. She'll like to hear you.

Pause. Al has put the lace around the back of his neck and pulled it tight against the plastic bag. He ties the knot in the lace.

Come on. Say something, Al. Do something. Make a noise. Any kind of noise will do. Grunt if you feel like grunting. Stamp your feet. Snap your fingers.

Pause. Al tightens the knot on the lace.

You can make some kind of sound. Come on. You could at least moan.

Claire isn't going to like this. You haven't grunted or done anything. You haven't made any kind of noise.

Al ties the knot firmly. Gerry holds the microphone in front of Al's contorted face inside the plastic bag.

The lights fade until only the hall light remains, spilling in a block into the living room. Gerry stands in the light from the hall while Al sits in relative darkness. Then blackout.

Other plays by Bryan Wade

NIGHTSHIFT
COFFEE BREAK
ANTI-GRAVITATIONAL MENOPAUSE
ALIENS
THIS SIDE OF THE ROCKIES
TANNED
BREAKTHROUGH

A BRIEF HISTORY OF THE SUBJECT
broadcast by CBC Television, 1975.